The Dark Night of the Soul
and
The Living Flame of Love

THE DARK NIGHT OF THE SOUL

and

THE LIVING FLAME OF LOVE

St John of the Cross

Fount

An Imprint of HarperCollins*Publishers*

Fount Paperbacks is an Imprint of
HarperCollins*Religious*
Part of HarperCollins*Publishers*
77–85 Fulham Palace Road, London W6 8JB

This edition first published in Great Britain
in 1995 by Fount Paperbacks

3   5   7   9   10   8   6   4   2

A catalogue record for this book is
available from the British Library

ISBN 0 00 627934 1

Printed and bound in Great Britain by
HarperCollinsManufacturing Glasgow

CONTENTS

The Dark Night of the Soul

BOOK II

OF THE NIGHT OF THE SPIRIT

The Living Flame of Love

Introduction

The diminutive figure of John of the Cross evoked extreme reactions in those he met. Some, like Teresa of Avila, adored him for his sharp intellect, his emotional intensity, and his uncompromising pursuit of what he believed to be right. Others resented and even hated him for those same qualities; and at a crucial point in his controversial career his enemies imprisoned him in a dark, airless room. It was in that room that he began to write the mystical works for which he remains famous, including *The Dark Night of the Soul.*

He was born in 1542 in Fontiveros, a small town in Castille. His father, Gonzalo, was from a rich family of silk merchants, probably of Jewish descent; but Gonzalo was disowned by his parents when he married Catalina, the daughter of a poor weaver. Soon after the marriage Gonzalo fell ill, and was able only to earn the most meagre living. They had three sons, of whom John was the youngest; but when John was three, Gonzalo's illness finally overcame him. Catalina and her three sons were plunged into dire poverty. They moved to Medina where at the age of nine John entered a school for poor children. He proved inept at the various manual trades the school tried to teach him, but loved caring for other children when they were sick. So he was transferred to a hospital where he worked as a nurse.

While at the hospital he began to attend classes in Latin and rhetoric at a nearby Jesuit school; and he soon shone as an outstanding pupil. At the age of twenty-one John was urged by the hospital administrator to seek ordination, and then take the post of chaplain at the hospital. But by now John was feeling called to a more contemplative life, and entered the Carmelite monastery in the city.

After a year he took vows as a Carmelite friar, and took the name of John of St Mary. The prior, recognizing his intellectual abilities, sent him to university at Salamanca, where the theological controversies of the day raged with particular passion. John enjoyed debate, and despite his youth proved equal to the most distinguished teachers there. In 1567 he was offered a post within the university, but again the call of the contemplative life was too strong, and he decided to return to the monastery at Medina.

There he met Teresa of Avila, who was visiting the city to recruit new members for the monasteries she was founding. She too was a Carmelite, but had rebelled against the laxness of her monastery, and started a much stricter monastery of her own. The Father General of the Carmelites, impressed by her reforms, had instructed her to form similar monasteries throughout Spain. These monasteries were known as 'discalced' because, like the original Carmelites three centuries earlier, the members wore no shoes. John was inspired by Teresa's vision, and she saw in him the person to extend her reforms to the male part of the Carmelite order. John spent a year living alongside the nuns in Teresa's monastery, observing and sharing their simple life of prayer and manual work. Then in 1568, with two other friars, John walked to Duruelo, a lonely village near his birthplace, to form the first reformed Carmelite community for men. He changed his own dedication to John of the Cross, to signify the physical hardship he and his brethren had accepted.

The community soon grew, and a second monastery for men was founded on the same lines. But in 1571 John himself was ordered by the Carmelite order to go to Avila, to act as spiritual director of the nuns there. He quickly became entangled in the politics of the Carmelites, and by extension the disputes engulfing the whole Spanish Church. The community where he lived was the one which Teresa herself had left. Teresa was now striving to persuade her original community to accept her reforms, and she saw John as an ally. The papal nuncio in Spain supported her; but when he died in 1577 those resisting the reforms seized the opportunity to try to stamp them out. John was arrested and taken blindfold to the monastery at

Tostado. There he was flogged, and then locked into a tiny room with only a small window high up on the wall. He was given only bread and water, and had no human company.

In these bleak circumstances he had the most profound experiences and visions of God; and he composed in his mind a number of mystical poems. After eight months John managed to escape. For the next two years he lived secretly, and began to write commentaries on the poems he had composed in prison. In 1580 the Pope decreed that the reformed Carmelite order under Teresa could break away from the rest, and form a separate religious order. John came out of hiding to become prior of a reformed monastery in Granada, and later of the monastery in Segovia. During this period he wrote his four great books, all of which are commentaries on poems he himself composed in prison.

He remained a controversial figure even within the reformed Carmelite order; and in 1591 he was voted out of office. Two friars, who resented his powerful spiritual influence, brought charges of misconduct against him, and an investigation began. John, however, fell ill with an inflamed leg. He went to the monastery at Ubeda for treatment, where the prior proved hostile to him, giving him only a bed and sparse rations. John's illness worsened rapidly, with the inflammation spreading across his body. Finally the prior relented, coming to John in tears to seek forgiveness for his harshness. But the repentance came too late to save John, and on 14 December he died.

The first two of John's books, *The Ascent of Mount Carmel* and *The Dark Night of the Soul*, concerned the stripping bare of the soul; and of these the latter is justly the more famous. John divides the dark night into two parts. Initially there is the 'night of sense' in which the self concentrates its desires on God alone rather than on any external objects. Then there is the 'night of spirit' in which the self is denied even spiritual pleasure and gratification; only then can the dawn of God's light begin to break. In both parts of the night there are both active and passive aspects: the soul has to strive for transparent honesty with itself, confronting not only its own sin but also any vestiges of self-satisfaction; equally it has to allow God total control.

John's second two books, *The Spiritual Canticle of the Soul* and *The Living Flame of Love*, concern the divine illumination which follows the dark night. He describes the sweetness, happiness and peace which the soul devoted to God experiences; but in the latter work he shows how ultimately the soul passes through these sensations to a bliss which is beyond sense and description. In both works there is erotic imagery to express the soul's relationship with God. But in *The Living Flame* the most striking images are those of suffering and joy: through union with God pain itself becomes a divine pleasure.

The Dark Night of the Soul is an original translation by Benedict Zimmerman, himself a Carmelite friar. *The Living Flame of Love* is translated by David Lewis and amended by Benedict Zimmerman.

Robert Van de Weyer

The Dark Night of the Soul

With an explanation of the stanzas
comprising the way of the perfect union of
love with God, such as is possible in this life;
and the admirable endowments of the soul
which has attained to it

ARGUMENT

The stanzas to be explained are set forth at the beginning of this book, then an explanation of each severally, the stanza being placed before it. After that an explanation of each line, which is also set before the explanation. The first two stanzas explain the two spiritual purgations of the sensual and spiritual part of man, and the other six the various and admirable effects of the spiritual enlightenment and union of love with God.

STANZAS

I

In a dark night,
With anxious love inflamed,
O, happy lot!
Forth unobserved I went,
My house being now at rest.

II

In darkness and safety,
By the secret ladder, disguised,
O, happy lot!
In darkness and concealment,
My house being now at rest.

III

In that happy night,
In secret, seen of none,
Seeing nought myself,
Without other light or guide
Save that which in my heart was burning.

IV

That light guided me
More surely than the noonday sun
To the place where He was waiting for me,
Whom I knew well,
And where none appeared.

V

O, guiding night;
O, night more lovely than the dawn;
O, night that hast united
The lover with His beloved,
And changed her into her love.

VI

On my flowery bosom,
Kept whole for Him alone,
There He reposed and slept;
And I cherished Him, and the waving
Of the cedars fanned Him.

VII

As His hair floated in the breeze
That from the turret blew,
He struck me on the neck
With His gentle hand,
And all sensation left me.

VIII

I continued in oblivion lost,
My head was resting on my love;
Lost to all things and myself,
And, amid the lilies forgotten,
Threw all my cares away.

EXPLANATION OF THE STANZAS

Before we enter on an explanation of these, it is right we should understand that they are the words of the soul already in the state of perfection, which is the union of love with God, when it has gone through the straits, tribulations and severities, by means of the spiritual training, of the strait way of everlasting life, by which ordinarily the soul attains to this high and divine union with God. Of it our Saviour says in the Gospel, 'How narrow is the gate and strait is the way that leadeth to life, and few there are that find it.' This road being so strait, and they who find it being so few, the soul regards it as a great and joyful blessing that it has journeyed on it to the perfection of love, as it sings in the first stanza, very rightly calling the strait road, a dark night, as may be seen further on in the words of the stanza. The soul, therefore, rejoicing in that it has travelled on this strait road whereby so great a blessing has come to it, sings as follows.

BOOK I

OF THE NIGHT OF SENSE

> *In a dark night,*
> *With anxious love inflamed,*
> *O, happy lot!*
> *Forth unobserved I went,*
> *My house being now at rest.*

In the first stanza the soul sings of the way and manner of its going forth, as to its affections, from self and all created things, dying thereto by real mortification, that it may live the life of love, sweet and delicious in God. It went forth, from itself and from all things, in a dark night, by which is meant here purgative contemplation – as I shall hereinafter explain – which causes in the soul passive denial of self and of all besides. This departure, it says, it was able to accomplish in the strength and fervour which the love of the Bridegroom supplied, in the obscure contemplation for that end. The soul magnifies its own happiness in having journeyed Godwards in that night so successfully as to escape all hindrance on the part of its three enemies – the world, the devil, and the flesh – which are always found infesting this road; for the night of purgative contemplation had lulled to sleep and mortified, in the house of sensuality, all passions and desires, in their rebellious movements.

CHAPTER I

Begins with the first stanza and treats of the imperfections
of beginners

1. Three states: beginners, proficients and perfect.
2. Beginners encouraged by sweetness.
3. Continuation.
4. Selfish spirituality of beginners. Work proportioned to
   habit.
5. Imperfections.

In a dark night,

Souls begin to enter the dark night when God is drawing them out of
the state of beginners, which is that of those who meditate on the
spiritual road, and is leading them into that of proficients, the state
of contemplatives, that, having passed through it, they may arrive at
the state of perfect, which is that of the divine union with God. That
we may the better understand and explain the nature of this night
through which the soul has to pass, and why God leads men into it, it
may be well to touch first upon certain peculiarities of beginners,
which, though treated in the briefest possible way, it is well for them
to know, that they may perceive the weakness of the state they are in,
take courage, and desire to be led of God into this night, where the
soul is established in virtue and made strong for the inestimable
delights of His love. Though I shall dwell at some length upon this
point, I shall do so no longer than suffices for the immediate discussion of this dark night.

2. We are to keep in mind that a soul, when seriously converted to

the service of God, is, in general, spiritually nursed and caressed, as an infant by its loving mother, who warms it in her bosom, nourishes it with her own sweet milk, feeds it with tender and delicate food, carries it in her arms, and fondles it. But as the child grows up the mother withholds her caresses, hides her breasts, and anoints them with the juice of bitter aloes; she carries the infant in her arms no longer, but makes it walk on the ground, so that, losing the habits of an infant, it may apply itself to greater and more substantial pursuits.

3. The grace of God, like a loving mother, as soon as the soul is regenerated in the new fire and fervour of His service, treats it in the same way; for it enables it, without labour on its own part, to find its spiritual milk, sweet and delicious, in all the things of God, and in devotional exercises great sweetness; God giving it the breasts of His own tender love, as to a tender babe. Such souls, therefore, delight to spend many hours, and perhaps whole nights, in prayer; their pleasures are penances, their joy is fasting, and their consolations lie in the use of the sacraments and in speaking of divine things.

4. Now spiritual men generally, speaking spiritually, are extremely weak and imperfect here, though they apply themselves to devotion, and practise it with great resolution, earnestness, and care. For being drawn to these things and to their spiritual exercises by the comfort and satisfaction they find therein, and not yet confirmed in virtue by the struggle it demands, they fall into many errors and imperfections in their spiritual life; for every man's work corresponds to the habit of perfection which he has acquired. These souls, therefore, not having had time to acquire those habits of vigour, must, of necessity, perform their acts, like children, weakly.

5. To make this more clear, and to show how weak are beginners in virtue in those good works which they perform with so much ease and pleasure, I proceed to explain by reference to the seven capital sins, pointing out some of the imperfections into which beginners fall in the matter of each of them. This will show us plainly how like children they are in all they do, and also how great are the blessings of this dark night of which I am about to speak; seeing that it cleanses and purifies the soul from all these imperfections.

CHAPTER II

Of some spiritual imperfections to which beginners are liable in the matter of pride

1. First imperfection: spiritual pride.
2. Fed by Satan.
3. Rebellion against confessors.
4. Deceitful confessions.
5. Pride of impatience with self.
6. Continuation.
7. Conduct of the humble beginner.
8-10. Marks of true, simple spirituality.
11. How the humble man bears his own imperfections.

When beginners become aware of their own fervour and diligence in their spiritual works and devotional exercises, this prosperity of theirs gives rise to secret pride – though holy things tend of their own nature to humility – because of their imperfections; and the issue is that they conceive a certain satisfaction in the contemplation of their works and of themselves. From the same source, too, proceeds that empty eagerness which they display to some extent, and occasionally very much, in speaking before others of the spiritual life, and sometimes as teachers rather than learners. They condemn others in their heart when they see that they are not devout in their way. Sometimes also they say it in words, showing themselves herein to be like the Pharisee, who in the act of prayer boasted of his own works and despised the Publican.

2. Their fervour, and desire to do these and other works, is

frequently fed by Satan in order that they may grow in pride and presumption: he knows perfectly well that all their virtue and works are not only nothing worth, but rather tending to sin. Some of them go so far as to desire none should be thought good but themselves, and so, at all times, both in word and deed fall into condemnation and detraction of others. They see the mote in the eye of their brother, but not the beam which is in their own. They strain out the gnat in another man's cup, and swallow the camel in their own.

3. Sometimes, also, when their spiritual masters, such as confessors and superiors, do not approve of their spirit and conduct – for they wish to be praised and considered for what they do – they decide that they are not understood, and that their superiors are not spiritual men because they do not approve and sanction their proceedings. So they go about in quest of some one else, who will accommodate himself to their fancy; for in general they love to discuss their spiritual state with those who, they think, will commend and respect it. They avoid, as they would death, those who destroy their delusion with the view of leading them into a safe way, and sometimes they even hate them. Presuming greatly on themselves, they make many resolutions, and accomplish little. They are occasionally desirous that others should perceive their spirituality and devotion, and for that end they give outward tokens by movements, sighs and divers ceremonies; sometimes, too, they fall into certain trances in public rather than in private – whereunto Satan contributes – and are pleased when others are witnesses of them.

4. Many of them seek to be the favourites of their confessors, and the result is endless envy and disquietude. They are ashamed to confess their sins plainly, lest their confessors should think less of them, so they go about palliating them, that they may not seem so bad; which is excusing rather than accusing themselves. Sometimes they go to a stranger to confess their sin, that their usual confessor may think they are not sinners, but good people. And so they always take pleasure in telling him of their goodness, and that in terms

suggestive of more than is in them: at the least, they wish all their goodness to be appreciated, when it would be greater humility on their part, as I shall presently show, to undervalue it, and wish that neither their confessor nor anyone else should think it of the least importance.

5. Some beginners, too, make light of their faults, and at other times indulge in immoderate grief when they commit them. They thought themselves already saints, and so they become angry and impatient with themselves, which is another great imperfection. They also importune God to deliver them from their faults and imperfections, but it is for the comfort of living in peace, unmolested by them, and not for God; they do not consider that, were He to deliver them, they would become, perhaps, prouder than ever. They are great enemies of other men's praise, but great lovers of their own, and sometimes they seek it. In this respect they resemble the foolish virgins, who, when their lamps gave no light, went about in search of oil, saying: 'Give us of your oil, for our lamps are going out.'

6. From these some go on to very serious imperfections, and come to great harm thereby. Some, however, fall into them less than others, and some have to contend with little more than the first movements of them. But scarcely anyone can be found who, in his first fervours, did not fall into some of them.

7. But those who at this time are going on to perfection proceed in a very different way, and in a very different temper of mind: they grow and are built up in humility, not only looking on their own works as nothing, but also dissatisfied with themselves; they look upon all others as much better, they regard them with a holy envy in their anxiety to serve God as they do. For the greater their fervour, the more numerous their good works; and the keener the pleasure therein, the more they perceive – for they humble themselves – how much that is which God deserves at their hands, and how little is all they can do for Him; thus the more they do, the less are they satisfied.

8. So great is that which they in their love would fain do, that all they are doing seems nothing. This loving anxiety so importunes

and fills them that they never consider whether others are doing good or not, and if they do, it is, as I have said, in the conviction that all others are much better than they are. They think little of themselves, and wish others to do so also, to make no account of them and despise their works. Moreover, if anyone should praise and respect them they will give them no credit, for they think it strange that anybody should speak well of them.

9. They, in great tranquillity and humility, are very desirous to learn the things that are profitable to them from anyone; in this respect the very opposite of those of whom I have just spoken, who are willing to teach everybody; and who, when anyone seems about to teach them anything, take the words out of his mouth, as if they knew it already.

10. But they of whom I am now speaking are very far from wishing to instruct anyone; they are most ready to travel by another road if they be but commanded, for they never imagine that they can be right in anything. When others are praised they rejoice, and their only regret is that they do not serve God themselves as well as they. They have no wish to speak about their own state, for they think so lightly of it, that they are ashamed to speak of it to their own confessors; it seems to them unworthy of any mention whatever. But they have a great desire to speak of their shortcomings and sins, which they would rather have known than their virtues: thus they incline to treat of the affairs of their soul with those who have no great opinion of their state and spirit. This is a characteristic of that spirituality which is pure, simple, true, and most pleasing unto God. For as the wise Spirit of God dwells in these humble souls, He moves and inclines them to keep His treasures secretly within, and to cast out the evil. For God gives this grace, together with the other virtues, to the humble, and withholds it from the proud.

11. These will give their hearts' blood for him who serves God, and will help him to serve Him to the utmost of their powers. When they fall into any imperfection they bear up under it with humility, in meekness of spirit, in loving fear of God, and hoping in Him. But the souls who in the beginning travel thus towards perfection are, as

I said, few, yea, very few, and we ought to be content when they do not rush into the opposite evils. This is the reason, as I shall hereafter explain, why God leads into the dark night those souls whom He will purify from all these imperfections in order to further their progress.

CHAPTER III

Of the imperfections into which some beginners are wont
to fall, in the matter of the second capital sin, which is
avarice, in the spiritual sense

1. Spiritual avarice.
2. Real devotion must spring from the heart.
3. Two examples of the spirit of poverty.
4. The humble man begins with generosity.
5. Real perfection, God alone can make Saints.

Many a beginner also falls at times into great spiritual avarice. Scarcely
anyone is contented with that measure of the spirit which God gives;
they are very disconsolate and querulous because they do not find the
comfort they desire in spiritual things. Many are never satisfied with
listening to spiritual counsels and precepts, with reading books which
treat of their state; and they spend more time in this than in doing
their duty, having no regard to that mortification, and perfection of
interior poverty of spirit to which they ought to apply themselves.
Besides, they load themselves with images, rosaries, and crucifixes,
curious and costly; now taking up one, then another, now changing
them, and then resuming them again. At one time they will have them
of a certain fashion, at another time of another, prizing one more than
another because more curious or costly. Some may be seen with an
Agnus Dei, and with relics and medals, like children with coral.

2. I condemn here that attachment and clinging of the heart to
the form, number, and variety of these things, because in direct
opposition to poverty of spirit, which looks only to the substance of

devotion; which makes use indeed of these things, but only sufficiently for the end, and disdains that variety and curiosity, for real devotion must spring out of the heart, and consider only the truth and substance which the objects in question represent. All beyond this is attachment and greed of imperfection; he who will go on unto perfection, must root out that feeling utterly.

3. I knew a person who for more than ten years used continually, without interruption, a cross rudely formed of a piece of blessed palm, and fastened together with a common pin bent backwards, until I took it away. This was a person not deficient in sense and understanding. I knew another who had a rosary made of the back-bones of fish, and whose devotion, I am certain, was not on that account of less value in the eyes of God; for it is clear that the cost or workmanship of these contributed nothing to it.

4. Those beginners, therefore, who go on well, do not rely on visible instruments, neither do they burden themselves with them, nor do they seek to know more than is necessary for acting rightly; their sole object is to be well with God and to please Him; their avarice consists in that. With a noble generosity they give up all they possess; and their delight is to be poor for the love of God and their neighbour, whether in matters spiritual or temporal; because, as I have said, their sole aim is real perfection, to please God in all things and themselves in nothing.

5. The soul, however, cannot be perfectly purified from these imperfections, any more than from the others, until God shall have led it into the passive purgation of the dark night, of which I shall speak immediately. But it is expedient that the soul, so far as it can, should labour, on its own part, to purify and perfect itself, that it may merit from God to be taken under His divine care, and be healed from those imperfections which of itself it cannot remedy. For, after all the efforts of the soul, it cannot by any exertions of its own actively purify itself so as to be in the slightest degree fit for the divine union of perfection in the love of God, if God Himself does not take it into His own hands and purify it in the fire, dark to the soul, in the way I am going to explain.

CHAPTER IV

Of other imperfections into which some beginners are
wont to fall, in the matter of the third sin, which is luxury,
spiritually understood

1. Spiritual luxury.
2. Continuation.
3. First source: sensible sweetness.
4. Law of the flesh and of the spirit.
5. Second source: the devil.
6. Continuation.
7. Third source: fear.
8. Continuation.
9. Test of purely spiritual affection.
10. Difference between human and divine love; in the
    Dark Night the affections are ruled by reason.

Many beginners fall into other imperfections, over and above those
belonging to each capital sin of which I am speaking. I pass them by
now, to avoid prolixity, and treat of some of the chiefest, which are, as
it were, the source and origin of the rest.

2. As to the sin of luxury, putting aside the commission of the sin
– my object being to speak of those imperfections which have to be
purged away in the dark night – beginners fall into many imperfections, which may be called spiritual luxury; not that it is so in fact,
but because, originating in spiritual things, it is felt and experienced
sometimes in the flesh, because of its frailty, when the soul is the
recipient of spiritual communications. For very often, in the midst

of their spiritual exercises, and when they cannot help themselves, the impure movements and disturbances of sensuality are felt; and sometimes even when the mind is absorbed in prayer, or when they are receiving the sacraments of penance and the eucharist. These movements, not being in their power, proceed from one of three sources.

3. They proceed occasionally – though but rarely, and in persons of delicate constitutions – from sensible sweetness in spiritual things. For when sense and spirit are both delighted together, the whole nature of man is moved in that delectation according to its measure and character. For then the spirit, that is, the higher part of our nature, is moved to delight itself in God; and sensuality, which is the lower part, is moved towards sensible gratification, because it knows, and admits of, none other, and therefore is moved to what lies nearest to it, namely sensual pleasure. And so it happens that the soul is in spirit praying, and on the other hand in the senses troubled, to its great disgust, with the rebellious movements and disturbances of the flesh passively; this happens often at the moment of communion, because when the soul receives at the hands of our Lord the happy consummation of love which God intends to bestow, the sensual nature, as we have seen, takes its share in its own manner. But inasmuch as these two parts form but one subject, man, they ordinarily share in their respective passions, each in its own way; for, as the philosopher tells us, all that is received is received according to the condition of the recipient.

4. Thus in these beginnings, and even when the soul has made some progress, the sensual part, being still imperfect, often receives the spirit of God with that very imperfection. But when the sensual part is already renewed in the purgation of the dark night, it is no longer subject to these infirmities, because it receives so abundantly of the Spirit of God that it seems rather to be received into that Spirit itself, 'as into that which is greater and grander'. Thus it possesses everything according to the measure of the Spirit, 'in an admirable manner, of Whom it is a partaker, united with God'.

5. The second source of these rebellious movements is Satan, who, in order to disquiet the soul during prayer, or when preparing for it, causes these filthy movements of our lower nature, and these, when in any degree admitted, are injury enough. Some persons not only relax in their prayers through fear of these movements, which is the object of Satan when he undertakes to assail them, but even abandon them altogether, for they imagine that they are more liable to these assaults during prayer than at other times. This is certainly true; for the devil then assails them more than at other times, that they may cease from prayer.

6. This is not all; for he represents before them then, most vividly, the most foul and filthy images, and occasionally in close relation with certain spiritual things and persons, by whom their souls are profited, that he may terrify and cow them. Some are so grievously assailed that they dare not dwell upon anything, for it becomes at once a stumbling-block to them, especially those who are of a melancholy temperament; these are so vehemently and effectually assailed as to be objects of the deepest pity; theirs, indeed, is a sad plight, for with some persons this trouble, when under the influence of melancholy, goes so far as to convince them that they hold communication with the evil spirit, which they are powerless to resist; some, nevertheless, with a supreme effort, tear themselves away. When melancholy is the occasion of these visitations of Satan, men in general cannot be delivered from them till their bodily health is improved, unless the dark night has overtaken the soul, gradually freeing it from all this trouble.

7. The third source of these depraved movements which war against the soul is usually the fear of them, for this fear which is brought about by a sudden remembrance of them, in a look, a word, or thought, makes souls suffer from them, but without fault on their part. Some souls, tender and fragile, never experience spiritual fervour or consolation in prayer without the spirit of luxury intruding at once and intoxicating their sensible nature until they are all but ingulfed in and subjugated by this vice, the disturbance lasting, passively, as long as the fervour and sometimes succeeding in

stirring the senses into rebellion. The reason is that these natures, as stated, are fragile and tender, and therefore susceptible to the slightest alteration of blood and humour whence these disturbances come, for exactly the same thing happens when they are roused to anger or upset by pain.

8. Sometimes, spiritual persons, when either speaking of spiritual things, or doing good works, display a certain energy and strength arising out of their consideration for persons present, and that with a certain measure of vain joy. This also proceeds from spiritual luxury in the sense in which I use the word, and is accompanied usually by a certain complacency of the will.

9. Some, too, from spiritual friendships with others, the source of which is luxury, and not spirituality. We may know it to be so by observing whether the remembrance of that affection increases our recollection and love of God, or brings remorse of conscience. When this affection is purely spiritual, the love of God grows with it, and the more we think of it the more we think of God, and the greater our longing for Him; for the one grows with the other. The Spirit of God has this property, that it increases good by good, because there is a likeness and conformity between them. But when this affection springs out of the vice of sensuality, its effects are quite opposite; for the more it grows, the more is the love of God diminished, and the remembrance of Him also; for if this earthly love grows, that of God cools down; the remembrance of that love brings forgetfulness of God and a certain remorse of conscience.

10. On the other hand, if the love of God grows in the soul, the human love cools, and is forgotten; for as they are contrary the one to the other, not only do they not help each other, but the one which predominates suppresses the other, and strengthens itself, as philosophers say. And so our Saviour tells us in the Gospel, saying, 'that which is born of the flesh is flesh, and that which is born of the spirit is spirit': that love which grows out of sensuality ends in the same, and that which is spiritual ends in the Spirit of God, and makes it grow. This is the difference between these two loves, whereby we may know them. When the soul enters the dark night,

these affections are ruled by reason; that night strengthens and purifies the affection which is according to God, and removes, destroys, or mortifies the other. In the beginning both are by it put out of sight, as I shall explain hereafter.

CHAPTER V

Of the imperfections of beginners in the matter of anger

1. Fourth imperfection: Anger and peevishness – how caused.
2. Impatience with self or others contrary to humility.
3. Saints not made in a day. *Festina lente*.

Many beginners, because of their inordinate appetite for spiritual sweetness, generally fall into many imperfections in the matter of anger; for when spiritual things minister to them no more sweetness and delight, they naturally become peevish, and in that bitterness of spirit prove a burden to themselves in all they do; trifles make them angry, and they are at times intolerable to all about them. This happens generally after great sweetness in prayer; and so, when that sensible sweetness is past, their natural temper is soured and rendered morose. They are like a babe weaned from the breast, which he found so sweet. When this natural feeling of displeasure is not permitted to grow, there is no sin, but only imperfection, which will have to be purged away in the severity and aridities of the dark night.

2. There are other spiritual persons, too, among these who fall into another kind of spiritual anger. They are angry with other people for their faults, with a sort of unquiet zeal, and watch them; they are occasionally moved to blame them, and even do so in anger, constituting themselves guardians of virtue. All this is contrary to spiritual meekness.

3. Others, again, seeing their own imperfections, become angry

with themselves with an impatience that is not humble. They are so impatient with their shortcomings as if they would be saints in one day. Many of these make many and grand resolutions, but, being self-confident and not humble, the more they resolve, the more they fall, and the more angry they become; not having the patience to wait for God's time; this is also opposed to spiritual meekness. There is no perfect remedy for this but in the dark night. There are, however, some people who are so patient, and who advance so slowly in their spiritual progress, that God wishes they were not so patient.

CHAPTER VI

Of the imperfections in the matter of spiritual gluttony

1. Fifth imperfection: spiritual gluttony.
2. Folly of exterior without interior mortification. Mortification of reason: obedience.
3. Obedience better than sacrifice.
4. Folly of self-direction.
5. Self-love in unadvised frequent communion.
6. Invisible grace better than sensible sweetness.
7. How some seek, not God, but themselves, even in prayer.
8. Continuation.
9. Desire for spiritual sweetness enfeebles the will. Spiritual sobriety.

There is much to say of the fourth capital sin, which is spiritual gluttony, for there is scarcely one among beginners, however good his progress, who, in the matter of this sin, does not fall into some of the many imperfections to which beginners are liable, because of that sweetness which in the beginning they find in spiritual exercises.

2. Many beginners, delighting in the sweetness and joy of their spiritual occupations, strive after spiritual sweetness rather than after purity and discretion, which is that which God regards and accepts in the whole course of the spiritual way. For this reason, over and above their imperfection in seeking after sweetness in devotion, that spirit of gluttony, which has taken possession of them, forces them to overstep the limits of moderation, within which virtue is

acquired and consists. For allured by the delights they then experience, some of them kill themselves by penances, and others weaken themselves by fasting. They take upon themselves more than they can bear, without rule or advice; they try to conceal their austerities from those whom they are bound to obey, and some even venture to practise them though commanded to abstain. These are full of imperfections – unreasonable people, who undervalue submission and obedience, which is the penance of the reason and judgment, and therefore a more acceptable and sweet sacrifice unto God than all the acts of bodily penance. Bodily penance which is nothing more than a suffering of the body and might as well be imposed on animals is full of imperfections when the penance of the will is neglected, for men undertake it merely because they like it, and for the sweetness which they find in it.

3. Inasmuch then as all extremes are vicious, and as in this course of conduct men follow their own will, the consequences are that they grow in vice and not in virtue; at least they minister to their spiritual gluttony and pride, for they do not walk in the way of obedience. The devil so deceives many of them by exciting their gluttony through this sweetness which he increases, that, since they cannot obey, they either change, or vary, or add to, what is commanded them; so hard and bitter is obedience become. The evil has so grown upon some, that they lose all desire to do their spiritual duties the instant obedience enjoins them; because all their satisfaction consists in doing that which pleases them, and perhaps it would be better for them to leave it undone.

4. Many of these importune their spiritual directors to allow them to do their own will: they extort that permission as if by force, and if it be refused, they mope like children, and become discontented, and think they are not serving God whenever they are thwarted. These persons clinging to sweetness and their own will, which they imagine is the will of God, the moment they are contradicted, and directed according to the will of God, become fretful, fainthearted, and then fall away. They imagine that to please and satisfy themselves, is to serve and please God.

5. Others also there are, who, by reason of this spiritual gluttony, are so ignorant of their own meanness and misery, and so insensible to that loving fear and reverence due to the majesty of God, that they are not afraid to insist on being allowed by their confessors to confess and communicate frequently. And what is much worse, they very often dare to communicate without the leave and sanction of the minister and steward of Christ, purely out of their own head, and hide the truth from him. This eagerness for communion makes them confess carelessly, for they are more anxious to communicate anyhow than to communicate in pureness and perfection. It would be more profitable for them, and a holier course, to beg their confessors not to enjoin such frequent communions; though the better way between these two extremes is to be humble and resigned. This excessive boldness leads to great evil, and men may well be in fear of chastisement for such rashness.

6. These persons, when they communicate, strive with all their might for sensible sweetness, instead of worshipping in humility and praising God within themselves. So much are they given to this, that they think when they derive no sensible sweetness, they have done nothing, so meanly do they think of God; neither do they understand that the least of the blessings of the Most Holy Sacrament is that which touches the senses, and that the invisible grace It confers is far greater; for God frequently withholds these sensible favours from men, that they may fix the eyes of faith upon Himself. But these persons will feel and taste God, as if He were palpable and accessible to them, not only in communion but in all their other acts of devotion. All this is a very great imperfection, being against the purity of Faith, and directly at variance with the nature of God.

7. They conduct themselves in the same way when they are praying; for they imagine that the whole business of prayer consists in sensible devotion, and this they strive to obtain with all their might, wearying out their brains and perplexing all the faculties of their souls. When they miss that sensible devotion, they are cast down, thinking they have done nothing. This effort after sweetness destroys true devotion and spirituality, which consist in perseverance in

prayer with patience and humility, mistrusting self, solely to please God. Therefore, when they once miss sweetness in prayer, or in any other act of religion, they feel a sort of repugnance to resume it, and sometimes cease from it altogether.

8. In this they are, as we said just now, like children who are not influenced by reason, but by their inclinations. They waste their time in the search after spiritual consolation, and are never satisfied with reading good books, taking up one meditation after another, in the pursuit of sensible sweetness in the things of God. God refuses it to them most justly, wisely, and lovingly, for if He did not, this spiritual gluttony on their part would grow into great evils. For this reason, it is most necessary that they should enter into the dark night, that they may be cleansed from this childishness.

9. They who are bent on sensible sweetness, labour also under another very great imperfection: excessive weakness and remissness on the rugged road of the cross; for the soul that is given to sweetness naturally sets its face against all the pain of self-denial. They labour under many other imperfections, which have their origin here, of which our Lord will heal them in due time, through temptations, aridities and trials, elements of the dark night. I will not enlarge upon them here, that I may avoid prolixity; but this will I say, that spiritual soberness and temperance produce a far different temper, that of mortification, of fear and submission in all things; showing us that the perfection and value of things consist not in the multitude thereof, but in our knowing how to deny ourselves in them. Spiritual men must labour after this with all their might, until it shall please God to purify them by leading them into the dark night. I hasten on with the description of these imperfections, that I may enter on the explanation of it.

Chapter VII

Of the imperfections in the matter of envy and spiritual sloth

1. Sixth and seventh imperfections: envy and spiritual sloth as against the holy envy of charity.
2. Cause and effects of spiritual sloth.
3. Perfection is to do the will of God.
4. Why prayer is sometimes irksome; true spiritual joys of the Cross.
5. Good fruits of the Dark Night; God alone can purify the soul.

Beginners are not free from many imperfections, in the matter of the two other vices, envy and spiritual sloth. Many of them are often vexed because of other men's goodness. They are sensibly afflicted when others outstrip them on the spiritual road, and will not endure to hear them praised. They become fretful over other men's virtues, and are sometimes unable to refrain from contradiction when they are commended; they depreciate them as much as they can, looking on them with an evil eye, and feel it acutely because they themselves are not thought so well of, for they wish to be preferred above all others. This is most opposed to that charity of which St Paul says, it 'rejoiceth with the truth'. If charity admits of envy at all, it is a holy envy that makes us grieve that we have not the virtues that others have; but still rejoicing that they have them, and glad that others outstrip us in the race that they may serve God, we being so full of imperfection ourselves.

2. As to spiritual sloth, beginners are wont to find their most spiritual occupations irksome, and avoid them as repugnant to their taste, for being so given to sweetness in spiritual things they loathe them when they find none. If they miss once this sweetness in prayer which is their joy – it is expedient that God should deprive them of it in order to try them – they will not resume it; at other times they omit it, or return to it with a bad grace. Thus, under the influence of sloth they neglect the way of perfection – which is the denial of their will and pleasure for God – for the gratification of their own will, which they serve rather than the will of God.

3. Many of these will have it that God should will that which they will, and are afflicted when they must will that which He wills, reluctantly submitting their own to the divine will. The result is that they frequently imagine that what is not according to their will is also not according to the will of God; and, on the other hand, when they are pleased, they believe that God is pleased. They measure Him by themselves, and not themselves by Him, in direct contradiction to His teaching in the Gospel; 'He that shall lose his life for My sake, shall find it.' That is, he who shall give up his will for God shall have it, and he who will have it, he shall have it never.

4. They also find it wearisome to obey when they are commanded to do that which they like not; and because they walk in the way of consolation and spiritual sweetness, they are too weak for the rough trials of perfection. They are like persons delicately nurtured who avoid with heavy hearts all that is hard and rugged, and are offended at the Cross wherein the joys of the spirit consist. The more spiritual the work they have to do, the more irksome do they feel it to be. And because they insist on having their own way and will in spiritual things, they enter on the 'strait way that leadeth unto life,' of which Christ speaks, with repugnance and heaviness of heart.

5. Let this reference to these imperfections among the many under which they labour, who are in the first state of beginners, suffice to show them how necessary it is that God should bring them to the state of proficients, which He effects when He leads them into the dark night of which we shall now speak. In that night He weans

them from the breasts of sweetness, in pure aridities and interior darkness, cleanses them from all these imperfections and childish ways, and by ways most different, makes them grow in virtue. For after all the exertions of beginners to mortify themselves in their actions and passions, their success will not be perfect, or even great, until God Himself shall do it for them in the purgation of the dark night. May God be pleased to give me His light, that I may speak profitably of this; for I have great need of it while treating of a night so dark and speaking of a subject so difficult.

CHAPTER VIII

Explanation of the first line of the first stanza. 'Beginning of the explanation of the dark night.'

1. The two nights.
2. The first more common than the second, but both painful.
3. How and why God sends the night of the senses.
4. Continuation.
5. Time and conditions of entering this night.

'In a dark night.' This night – it is contemplation – produces in spiritual men two sorts of darkness or purgations conformable to the two divisions of man's nature into sensual and spiritual. Thus the first night, or sensual purgation, wherein the soul is purified or detached, will be of the senses, subjecting them to the spirit. The other is that night or spiritual purgation wherein the soul is purified and detached in the spirit, and which subdues and disposes it for union with God in love. The night of sense is common, and the lot of many: these are the beginners, of whom I shall first speak. The spiritual night is the portion of very few; and they are those who have made some progress, exercised therein, of whom I shall speak hereafter.

2. The first night, or purgation, is bitter and terrible to sense. The second is not to be compared with it, for it is much more awful to the spirit, as I shall soon show. But as the night of sense is the first in order and the first to be entered, I shall speak of it briefly – for being

of ordinary occurrence, it is the matter of many treatises – that I may pass on to treat more at large of spiritual night; for of that very little has been said, either by word of mouth or in writing, and little is known of it even by experience.

3. But the behaviour of these beginners on the way of God is not noble, and very much according to their own liking and self-love, as I have said before. Meanwhile, God seeks to raise them higher, to draw them out of this miserable manner of loving to a higher state of the love of God, to deliver them from the low usage of the senses and meditation whereby they seek after God, as I said before, in ways so miserable and so unworthy of Him. He seeks to place them in the way of the spirit wherein they may the more abundantly, and more free from imperfections, commune with God now that they have been for some time tried in the way of goodness, persevering in meditation and prayer, and because of the sweetness they found therein have withdrawn their affections from the things of this world, and gained a certain spiritual strength in God, whereby they in some measure curb their love of the creature, and are able, for the love of God, to carry a slight burden of dryness, without going back to that more pleasant time when their spiritual exercises abounded in delights, and when the sun of the divine graces shone, as they think, more clearly upon them. God is now changing that light into darkness, and sealing up the door of the fountain of the sweet spiritual waters, which they tasted in God as often and as long as they wished. For when they were weak and tender, this door was then not shut, as it is written, 'Behold, I have given before thee an opened door, which no man can shut; because thou hast a little strength, and hast kept My word, and hast not denied My name.'

4. God thus leaves them in darkness so great that they know not whither to betake themselves with their imaginations and reflections of sense. They cannot advance a single step in meditation, as before, the inward sense now being overwhelmed in this night, and abandoned to dryness so great that they have no more any joy or sweetness in their spiritual exercises, as they had before; and in their place they find nothing but insipidity and bitterness. For, as I said before,

God now, looking upon them as somewhat grown in grace, weans them from the breasts that they may become strong, and cast their swaddling-clothes aside: He carries them in His arms no longer, and shows them how to walk alone. All this is strange to them, for all things seem to go against them.

5. Recollected persons enter the dark night sooner than others, after they have begun their spiritual course; because they are kept at a greater distance from the occasions of falling away, and because they correct more quickly their worldly desires, which is necessary in order to begin to enter the blessed night of sense. In general, there elapses no great length of time after they have begun before they enter the night of sense, and most of them do enter it, for they generally suffer aridities. The Holy Scriptures throughout, but especially the Psalms and the prophetical books, furnish many illustrations of the night of sense, for it is so common; but, to avoid prolixity, I omit them for the present, for those who do not see them there must content themselves with the general experience.

CHAPTER IX

Of the signs by which it may be known that the spiritual man is walking in the way of this night or purgation of sense

1. Three tests to distinguish the sensitive night from sin, tepidity or bodily weakness.
2. First test: absence of delight in creatures.
3. Second test: longing anxiety for God.
4. Difference between aridity and lukewarmness. Melancholy and other physical causes.
5. Purgative aridity, how and why produced.
6. The sensitive appetite like the Israelites in the wilderness.
7. The will strengthened by sensible aridity.
8. Peace found in humble resignation.
9. Continuation.
10. Reason of it.
11. Third test: inability to meditate by imagination and discursive reflection.
12. Continuation.
13. Not all spiritual persons reach contemplation.

But as these aridities frequently proceed, not from this night and purgation of the sensitive appetite, but from sins or imperfections, from weakness or lukewarmness, from some physical derangement or bodily indisposition, we shall here propose certain tests by which we may ascertain whether a particular aridity proceeds from the purgation of sense, or from any one of the vices I have just enumerated. There are three chief tests for this purpose:

2. The first is this: when we find no comfort in the things of God, and none also in created things. For when God brings the soul into the dark night in order to wean it from sweetness and to purge the desire of sense, He does not allow it to find sweetness or comfort anywhere. It is then possible, in such a case, that this dryness is not the result of sins or of imperfections recently committed; for if it were, we should feel some inclination or desire for other things than those of God. Whenever we give the reins to our desires in the way of any imperfection, our desires are instantly attracted to it, much or little, in proportion to the affection for it. But still, inasmuch as this absence of pleasure in the things of heaven and of earth may proceed from bodily indisposition or a melancholy temperament, which frequently cause dissatisfaction with all things, the second test and condition become necessary.

3. The second test and condition of this purgation are that the memory dwells ordinarily upon God with a painful anxiety and carefulness, the soul thinks it is not serving God, but going backwards, because it is no longer conscious of any sweetness in the things of God. In that case it is clear that this weariness of spirit and aridity are not the results of weakness and lukewarmness; for the peculiarity of lukewarmness is the want of earnestness in, and of interior solicitude for, the things of God.

4. There is, therefore, a great difference between dryness and lukewarmness, for the latter consists in great remissness and weakness of will and spirit, in the want of all solicitude about serving God. The true purgative aridity is accompanied in general by a painful anxiety, because the soul thinks that it is not serving God. Though this be occasionally increased by melancholy or other infirmity – so it sometimes happens – yet it is not for that reason without its purgative effects on the desires, because the soul is deprived of all sweetness, and its sole anxieties are referred to God. For when mere bodily indisposition is the cause, all that it does is to produce disgust and the ruin of bodily

health, without the desire of serving God which belongs to the purgative aridity. In this aridity, though the sensual part of man be greatly depressed, weak and sluggish in good works, by reason of the little satisfaction they furnish, the spirit is, nevertheless, ready and strong.

5. The cause of this dryness is that God is transferring to the spirit the goods and energies of the senses, which, having no natural fitness for them, become dry, parched up, and empty; for the sensual nature of man is helpless in those things which belong to the spirit simply. Thus the spirit having tasted, the flesh becomes weak and remiss; but the spirit, having received its proper nourishment, becomes strong, more vigilant and careful than before, lest there should be any negligence in serving God. At first it is not conscious of any spiritual sweetness and delight, but rather of aridities and distaste, because of the novelty of the change. The palate accustomed to sensible sweetness looks for it still. And because the spiritual palate is not prepared and purified for so delicious a taste until it shall have been for some time disposed for it in this arid and dark night, it cannot taste of the spiritual good, but rather of aridity and distaste, because it misses that which it enjoyed so easily before.

6. These, whom God begins to lead through the solitudes of the wilderness, are like the children of Israel, who, though God began to feed them, as soon as they were in the wilderness, with the manna of heaven, which was so sweet that as it is written, it turned to what every man liked, were more sensible to the loss of the onions and flesh of Egypt — for they liked them and had revelled in them — than to the delicious sweetness of the angelical food. So they wept and bewailed the flesh-pots of Egypt, saying, 'We remember the fish that we ate in Egypt free-cost; the cucumbers come into our mind, and the melons, and the leeks, and the onions, and the garlic.' Our appetite becomes so depraved that we long for miserable trifles, and loathe the priceless gifts of heaven.

7. But when these aridities arise in the purgative way of the sensual appetite, the spirit, though at first without any sweetness, for the reasons I have given, is conscious of strength and energy to act because of the substantial nature of its interior food, which is the

commencement of contemplation, dim and dry to the senses. This contemplation is in general secret, and unknown to him who is admitted into it, and with the aridity and emptiness which it produces in the senses, it makes the soul long for solitude and quiet, without the power of reflecting on anything distinctly, or even desiring to do so.

8. Now, if they who are in this state knew how to be quiet, to disregard every interior and exterior work – 'for the accomplishment of which they labour,' – to be without solicitude about everything, 'and resign themselves into the hands of God, with a loving interior obedience to His voice,' they would have, in this tranquillity, a most delicious sense of this interior food. This food is so delicate that, in general, it eludes our perceptions if we make any special effort to feel it, for, as I am saying, it does its work when the soul is most tranquil and free; it is like the air which vanishes when we shut our hands to grasp it.

9. The words of the bridegroom which, addressed to the bride, in the Canticles, are applicable to this matter: 'Turn away thine eyes from me, for they have made me flee away.' For this is God's way of bringing the soul into this state; the road by which He leads it is so different from the first, that if it will do anything in its own strength, it will hinder rather than aid His work. It was far otherwise once.

10. The reason is this: God is now working in the soul, in the state of contemplation, that is, when it advances from meditation to the state of proficients, in such a way as to seem to have bound up all the interior faculties, leaving no help in the understanding, no sweetness in the will, no reflections in the memory. Therefore, at this time, all that the soul can do of itself ends, as I have said, in disturbing the peace and the work of God in the spirit amid the dryness of sense. This peace, being spiritual and delicate, effects a work that is quiet and delicate, unobtrusive and satisfactory, pacific and utterly alien from the former delights, which were most gross and sensual. This is that peace, according to the Psalmist, which God speaks in the soul to make it spiritual. 'He will speak peace unto His people.' This brings us to the third test.

11. The third sign we have for ascertaining whether this dryness

be the purgation of sense, is inability to meditate and make reflections, and to excite the imagination, as before, notwithstanding all the efforts we may make; for God begins now to communicate Himself, no longer through the channel of sense, as formerly, in consecutive reflections, by which we arranged and divided our knowledge, but in pure spirit, which admits not of successive reflections, and in the act of pure contemplation, to which neither the interior nor the exterior senses of our lower nature can ascend. Hence it is that the fancy and the imagination cannot help or suggest any reflections, nor use them ever afterwards.

12. It is understood here that this embarrassment and dissatisfaction of the senses do not arise out of any bodily ailment. When they arise from this, the indisposition, which is always changeable, having ceased, the powers of the soul recover their former energies, and find their previous satisfactions at once. It is otherwise in the purgation of the appetite, for as soon as we enter upon this, the inability to make our meditations continually grows. It is true that this purgation at first is not continuous in some persons, for they are not altogether without sensible sweetness and comfort – their weakness renders their rapid weaning inexpedient – nevertheless, it grows upon them more and more, and the operations of sense diminish; if they are going on to perfection. They, however, who are not walking in the way of contemplation, meet with a very different treatment, for the night of aridities is not continuous with them, they are sometimes in it, and sometimes not; they are at one time unable to meditate, and at another able as before.

13. God leads these persons into this night only to try them and to humble them, and to correct their desires, that they may not grow up spiritual gluttons, and not for the purpose of leading them into the way of the spirit, which is contemplation. God does not raise to perfect contemplation every one that is tried in the way of the spirit, nor even half of them, and He alone knoweth why. Hence it is that these persons are never wholly weaned from the breasts of meditations and reflections, but only, as I have said, at intervals and at certain seasons.

CHAPTER X

How they are to conduct themselves who have entered the
Dark Night

1. Cause of the afflictions of the sensitive night.
2. Continuation.
3. Necessity of right instruction.
4. Confidence in God.
5. Conduct to be observed: patience and perseverance.
   The repose of love.
6. God will do His own work in the soul.
7. Continuation.
8. Meditation on the life and passion of Christ; contemplation an infusion of God.

During the aridities, then, of the night of sense – when God effects the change of which I have spoken, drawing the soul out of the way of sense into that of the spirit, from meditation to contemplation, where it is helpless in the things of God, so far as its own powers are concerned, as I have said – spiritual persons have to endure great afflictions, not so much because of aridity, but because they are afraid that they will be lost on this road; thinking that they are spiritually ruined, and that God has forsaken them, because they find no help or consolation in holy things. Under these circumstances, they weary themselves, and strive, as they were wont, to fix the powers of the soul with some satisfaction upon some matter of meditation, imagining when they cannot do this, and are conscious of the effort, that they are doing nothing. This they do not without great dislike and inward unwillingness on the part of the soul, which enjoys its state of quietness and rest, the faculties not being at work.

2. In thus turning away from this state they make no progress in the other, because, by exerting their own spirit, they lose that spirit which they had, that of tranquillity and peace. They are like a man who does his work over again; or who goes out of a city that he may enter it once more; or who lets go what he has caught in hunting that he may hunt it again. Their labour is in vain; for they will find nothing, and that because they are turning back to their former ways, as I have said already.

3. Under these circumstances, if they meet with no one who understands the matter, these persons fall away, and abandon the right road; or become weak, or at least put hindrances in the way of their further advancement, because of the great efforts they make to proceed in their former way of meditation, fatiguing their natural powers beyond measure. They think that their state is the result of negligence or of sin. All their own efforts are now in vain, because God is leading them by another and a very different road, that of contemplation. Their first road was that of discursive reflection, but the second knows no imagination or reasoning.

4. It behoves those who find themselves in this condition to take courage, and persevere in patience. Let them not afflict themselves, but put their confidence in God, who never forsakes those who seek Him with a pure and upright heart. Neither will He withhold from them all that is necessary for them on this road until He brings them to the clear and pure light of love, which He will show them in that other dark night of the spirit, if they shall merit an entrance into it.

5. The conduct to be observed in the night of sense is this: in nowise have recourse to meditations, for, as I have said, the time is now past, let the soul be quiet and at rest, though they may think they are doing nothing, that they are losing time, and that their lukewarmness is the reason of their unwillingness to employ their thoughts. They will do enough if they keep patience, and persevere in prayer; all they have to do is to keep their soul free, unembar-

rassed, and at rest from all thoughts and all knowledge, not anxious about their meditation, contenting themselves simply with directing their attention lovingly and calmly towards God; and all this without anxiety or effort, or desire to feel and taste His presence. For all such efforts disquiet the soul, and distract it from the calm repose and sweet tranquillity of contemplation to which they are now admitted.

6. And though they may have many scruples that they are wasting time, and that it may be better for them to betake themselves to some other good work, seeing that in prayer and meditation they are become helpless; yet let them be patient with themselves, and remain quiet, for that which they are uneasy about is their own satisfaction and liberty of spirit. If they were now to exert their inferior faculties, they would simply hinder and ruin the good which, in that repose, God is working in the soul; for if a man while sitting for his portrait cannot be still, but moves about, the painter will never depict his face, and even the work already done will be spoiled.

7. In the same way when the soul interiorly rests, every action and passion, or consideration at that time, will distract and disturb it, and make it feel the dryness and emptiness of sense. The more it strives to find help in affections and knowledge, the more will it feel the deficiency which cannot now be supplied in that way. It is therefore expedient for the soul which is in this condition not to be troubled because its faculties have become useless, yea, rather it should desire that they may become so quickly; for by not hindering the operation of infused contemplation, to which God is now admitting it, the soul is refreshed in peaceful abundance, and set on fire with the spirit of love, which this contemplation, dim and secret, induces and establishes within it.

8. Still, I do not mean to lay down a general rule for the cessation from meditation; that should occur when meditation is no longer feasible, and only then, when our Lord, either in the way of purgation and affliction, or of the most perfect contemplation, shall make it impossible. At other times, and on other occasions, this help must be had recourse to, namely, meditation on the life and passion of

Christ, which is the best means of purification and of patience and of security on the road, and an admirable aid to the highest contemplation. Contemplation is nothing else but a secret, peaceful, and loving infusion of God, which, if admitted, will set the soul on fire with the spirit of love, as I shall show in the explanation of the following verse.

CHAPTER XI

Explanation of the Second Line of the First Stanza

1. Second line of the first stanza. Earnest longing for God.
2. Martyrdom of divine love.
3. Love not felt at first, but after suffering.
4. Third line.
5. Fourth line: the escape from the sensitive appetite.
6. Continuation.
7. Happiness of leaving the creature for the Creator.
8. Continuation.

With anxious love inflamed,

The burning fire of love, in general, is not felt at first, for it has not begun to burn, either because of our natural impurity, or because the soul, not understanding its own state, has not given it, as I have said, a peaceful rest within. Sometimes, however, whether it be so or not, a certain longing after God begins to be felt; and the more it grows, the more the soul feels itself touched and inflamed with the love of God, without knowing or understanding how or whence that love comes, except that at times this burning so inflames it that it longs earnestly after God. David in this night said of himself, 'My heart is inflamed, and my reins are changed, and I am brought to nothing, and knew not.' That is, 'my heart hath been inflamed' in the love of contemplation; 'my reins', that is, my affections also, have been changed from the sensual to the spiritual way by this holy dryness, and in my denial of them, and 'I am brought to nothing, and I knew not.' The soul, as I have just said, not knowing the way it goeth, sees itself brought to nothing as to all things of heaven and earth, wherein it delighted before, and on fire with love, not knowing how.

2. And because occasionally this fire of love grows in the spirit greatly, the longings of the soul for God are so deep that the very bones seem to dry up in that thirst, the bodily health to wither, the natural warmth and energies to perish in the intensity of that thirst of love. The soul feels it to be a living thirst. So was it with David when he said, 'My soul hath thirsted after God, the living.' It is as if he had said, the thirst of my soul is a living thirst. We may say of this thirst, that, being a living thirst, it kills. Though it should be noted that this thirst is not continuously, but only occasionally, violent, nevertheless it is always felt in some degree.

3. I commenced by observing that this love, in general, is not felt at first, but only the dryness and emptiness of which I am speaking; and then, instead of love, which is afterwards enkindled, what the soul feels in the dryness and the emptiness of its faculties is a general painful anxiety about God, and a certain painful misgiving that it is not serving Him. But a soul anxious and afflicted for His sake is a sacrifice not a little pleasing unto God. Secret contemplation keeps the soul in this state of anxiety, until, in the course of time, having purged the sensual nature of man, in some degree, of its natural forces and affections by means of the aridities it occasions, it shall have kindled within it this divine love. But in the meantime, like a sick man in the hands of his physician, all it has to do, in the dark night and dry purgation of the desire, is to suffer, healing its many imperfections and practising many virtues, that it may become meet for the divine love, of which I shall speak while explaining the following line:

O happy lot!

4. When God establishes the soul in the dark night of sense, that He may purify, prepare, and subdue its lower nature, and unite it to the spirit, by depriving it of light, and causing it to cease from

meditation – as He afterwards establishes it also in the spiritual night, that He may purify the spirit, and prepare it for union with Himself – the soul makes a gain so great, though it does not think so, that it looks upon it as great happiness to have escaped from the bondage of the senses of its lower nature in that happy night, and therefore it sings – 'O happy lot!'

5. It is necessary now for us to point out the benefits which accrue to the soul in this night, and for the sake of which it pronounces itself happy in having passed through it. All these benefits are comprised in these words:

Forth unobserved I went,

6. This going forth of the soul is to be understood of that subjection to sense under which it laboured when it was seeking after God in such weak, narrow, and fitful ways, as are the ways of man's lower nature. It then fell at every step into a thousand imperfections and ignorances, as I showed while speaking of the seven capital sins, from all of which the spiritual man is delivered in the dark night which quenches all desire in all things whatsoever, and deprives him of all his lights in meditation, and brings with it other innumerable blessings in the acquirement of virtue, as I shall now show.

7. It will be a great joy and comfort to him who travels on this road, to observe how that which seemed so rugged and harsh, so contrary to spiritual sweetness, works in him so great a good. This good flows from going forth, as I am saying, as to all affections and operations of the soul, from all created things, in this night, and journeying towards those which are eternal, which is a great happiness and a great good. In the first place, because the desires are extinguished in all things; and in the second place, because they are few who persevere and enter in through the narrow gate, by the strait way that leadeth to life: 'How narrow is the gate and strait is the way that leadeth to life, and few there are that find it!' are words of our Lord.

8. The narrow gate is this night of sense. The soul detaches itself from sense that it may enter on it, basing itself on faith, which is a

stranger to all sense, that it may afterwards travel along the strait road of the other night of the spirit, by which it advances towards God in most pure faith, which is the means of union with Him. This road, because so strait, dark, and terrible – for there is no comparison, as I shall show, between its trials and darkness and those of the night of sense – is travelled by very few, but its blessings are so much the more. I shall begin now to say somewhat, with the utmost brevity, of the blessings of the night of sense, that I may pass on to the other.

CHAPTER XII

Of the benefits which the night of sense brings to the soul

1. Joy at the weaning of the soul from the goods of the sensitive appetite.
2. Benefits of the night of sense: infused contemplation.
3. Continuation.
4. Second benefit: knowledge of our own vileness.
5. Continuation.
6. Third benefit: reverence for God. Example of Moses.
7. Example of Job.
8. Spiritual illumination.
9. Isiais.
10. David.
11. Continuation.
12. Humility.
13. Love of our neighbours.
14. Docility.

This night and purgation of the appetite is full of happiness to the soul, involving grand benefits, though, as I have said, it seems to it as if all were lost. As Abraham made a great feast on the day of Isaac's weaning, so there is joy in heaven when God takes a soul out of its swaddling clothes; when He takes His arms from under it, and makes it walk alone; when He denies it the sweet milk of the breast and the delicate food of children, and gives it bread with the crust to eat; when it begins to taste the bread of the strong, which, in the aridities and darkness of sense, is given to the spirit emptied and dried of all sensible sweetness; namely, the bread of infused contemplation, of which I have spoken. This is the first and chief benefit which the soul gains here, and from which almost all the others flow.

2. Of these, the first is the knowledge of self and its own vileness. For over and above that those graces which God bestows on the soul are ordinarily included in this knowledge of self, these aridities and the emptiness of the faculties as to their former abounding, and the difficulty which good works present, bring the soul to a knowledge of its own vileness and misery, which in the season of prosperity it saw not. This truth is vividly shadowed forth in the book of Exodus. There we read that God, about to humble the children of Israel and bring them to a knowledge of themselves, commanded them to lay aside their ornaments and festival attire, which they ordinarily wore in the wilderness, saying, 'Now, lay aside thy ornaments'; that is, lay aside thy festival attire, and put on thy working dress, that thou mayest know what treatment thou hast deserved.

3. It is as if He said to the people: 'Inasmuch as the ornaments you wear, being those of joy and festivity, are the cause why you think not meanly of yourselves – you really are mean – lay them aside; so that henceforth clad in vile garments, you may acknowledge that you deserve nothing better, and also who and what you are.'

4. Hereby the soul learns the reality of its own misery, which before it knew not. For in the day of festivity when it found great sweetness, comfort, and help in God, it was highly satisfied and pleased, thinking that it rendered some service to God. For though it may not then explicitly say so, yet, on account of the satisfaction it finds, it is not wholly free from feeling it. But when it has put on the garments of heaviness, of aridity and abandonment, when its previous lights have become darkness, it possesses and retains more truly that excellent and necessary virtue of self-knowledge, counting itself for nothing, and having no satisfaction in itself, because it sees that of itself it does and can do nothing.

5. This diminished satisfaction with self, and the affliction it feels because it thinks that it is not serving God, God esteems more

highly than all its former delights and all its good works, however great they may have been; for they were occasions of many imperfections and ignorances. But in this garb of aridity, not only these, of which I am speaking, but other benefits also of which I shall presently speak, and many more than I can speak of, flow as from their proper source and fount, that of self-knowledge.

6. In the first place, the soul learns to commune with God with more respect and reverence; always necessary in converse with the Most High. Now, in its prosperous days of sweetness and consolation, the soul was less observant of reverence, for the favours it then received rendered the desire somewhat bold with God, and less reverent than it should have been. Thus it was with Moses, when he heard the voice of God; for carried away by the delight he felt, he was venturing, without further consideration, to draw near, if God had not commanded him to stop, and put off his shoes, saying, 'Come not nigh hither; put off the shoes from thy feet.' This teaches us how reverently and discreetly in spiritual detachment we are to converse with God. When Moses had become obedient to the voice, he remained so reverent and considerate, that not only did he not venture to draw near, but, in the words of Scripture, 'durst not look at God.' For having put off the shoes of desire and sweetness, he recognized profoundly his own wretchedness in the sight of God, for so it became him when about to listen to the words of God.

7. Again, the condition to which God brought Job in order that he might converse with God, was not that of delight and bliss, of which he there speaks, and to which he had been accustomed. God left him in misery, naked on a dung-hill, abandoned and even persecuted by his friends, killed with bitterness and grief, covered with worms: then it was that the Most High, Who lifteth up 'the poor out of the dung-hill,' was pleased to descend and speak to Job face to face, revealing to him 'the deep mysteries of His wisdom,' as He had never done before in the days of Job's prosperity.

8. And now that I have to speak of it, I must here point out another great benefit of the dark night and aridity of the sensual appetite; the fulfilment of the words of the prophet, 'Thy light shall

rise up in darkness.' God enlightens the soul, making it see not only its own misery and meanness, as I have said, but also His grandeur and majesty. When the desires are quelled, and sensible joy and consolation withdrawn, the understanding remains free and clear for the reception of the truth, for sensible joy and the desire even of spiritual things darken and perplex the mind, but the trials and aridities of sense also enlighten and quicken the understanding in the words of Isaias, 'Vexation alone shall give understanding in the hearing.' Vexation shall make us understand how God in His divine wisdom proceeds to instruct a soul, emptied and cleansed – for such it must be before it can be the recipient of the divine inflowing – in a supernatural way, in the dark and arid night of contemplation, which He did not do, because it was given up to its former sweetness and joy.

9. The same prophet Isaias sets this truth before us with great clearness, saying, 'Whom shall he teach knowledge? and whom shall he make to understand the thing heard? Them that are weaned from the milk, that are plucked away from the breasts.' The temper of mind, then, meet for the divine inflowing is not so much the milk of spiritual sweetness, nor the breasts of sweet reflections in the powers of sense, which the soul once had, as a failure of the first and withdrawal from the other. Therefore, if we would listen to the voice of God with due reverence, the soul must stand upright, and not lean on the affections of sense for support. As the prophet Habacuc said of himself, 'I will stand upon my watch, and fix my step upon the munition, and I will behold to see what may be said to me.' To stand upon the watch, is to cast off all desires; to fix the step, is to cease from reflections of sense, that I may behold and understand what God will speak to me. Thus out of this night springs first the knowledge of one's self, and on that, as on a foundation, is built up the knowledge of God. 'Let me know myself,' saith St Augustine, 'and I shall then know Thee, O my God,' for, as the philosophers say, one extreme is known by another.

10. In order to show more fully how effectual is the night of sense, in its aridity and desolation, to enlighten the soul more and more, I

produce here the words of the Psalmist, which so clearly explain how greatly efficacious is this night in bringing forth the knowledge of God: 'In a desert land, and inaccessible, and without water; so in the holy have I appeared to Thee, that I might see Thy strength and Thy glory.' The Psalmist does not say here – and it is worthy of observation – that his previous sweetness and delight were any dispositions or means whereby he might come to the knowledge of the glory of God, but rather that aridity and emptying of the powers of sense spoken of here as the barren and dry land.

11. Moreover, he does not say that his reflections and meditations on divine things, with which he was once familiar, had led him to the knowledge and contemplation of God's power, but, rather, his inability to meditate on God, to form reflections by the help of his imagination; that is the inaccessible land. The means, therefore, of attaining to the knowledge of God, and of ourselves, is the dark night with all its aridities and emptiness; though not in the fulness and abundance of the other night of the spirit; for the knowledge that comes by this is, as it were, the beginning of the other.

12. Amid the aridities and emptiness of this night of the desires, the soul acquires also spiritual humility, which is the virtue opposed to the first capital sin, which, I said, is spiritual pride. The humility acquired by self-knowledge purifies the soul from all the imperfections into which it fell in the day of its prosperity. For now, seeing itself so parched and miserable, it does not enter into its thoughts, even for a moment, to consider itself better than others, or that it has outstripped them on the spiritual road, as it did before; on the contrary, it acknowledges that others are better.

13. Out of this grows the love of our neighbour, for it now esteems them, and no longer judges them as it used to do, when it looked upon itself as exceedingly fervent, and upon others as not. Now it sees nothing but its own misery, which it keeps so constantly before its eyes that it can look upon nothing else. This state is admirably shown by David himself, when in this dark night, saying, 'I was dumb, and was humbled, and kept silence from good things, and my sorrow was renewed.' All the good of his soul seemed to him

so mean that he could not speak of it; he was silent as to the good of others, because of the pain of the knowledge of his own wretchedness.

14. In this state, too, men are submissive and obedient in the spiritual way, for when they see their own wretchedness they not only listen to instruction, but desire to have it from any one who will guide their steps and tell them what they ought to do. That selfish presumption which sometimes possessed them in their prosperity is now gone; and, finally, all those imperfections are swept clean away to which I referred when I was treating of spiritual pride.

CHAPTER XIII

Of other benefits which the night of sense brings to the soul

1. Liberty of spirit.
2. Spiritual purity.
3. Spiritual sobriety.
4. Spiritual temperance.
5. Holy fear of God.
6. Patience, love and peace.
7. Continuation.
8. Gentleness with God, self, and others. Holy emulation.
9. Fortitude amid aridities.
10. Other benefits.
11. Twelve fruits of the Holy Ghost.
12. Effects.
13. Anxious desire for the service of God.
14. Last benefit: deliverance from the world, the flesh, and the devil.
15. The 'house being set in order'.

The imperfections of spiritual avarice, under the influence of which the soul coveted this and that spiritual good, and was never satisfied with this or that practice of devotion, because of its eagerness for the sweetness it found therein, become now, in this arid and dark night, sufficiently corrected. For when the soul finds no sweetness and delight, as it was wont to do, in spiritual things, but rather bitterness and vexation, it has recourse to them with such moderation as to lose now, perhaps, through defect, what it lost before, through excess. Though, in general, to those who are brought to this night, God gives humility and readiness, but without sweetness, in order that they may obey Him solely through love. Thus they detach themselves from many things, because they find no sweetness in them.

2. The soul is purified, also, from those impurities of spiritual luxury of which I have spoken before, in this aridity and bitterness of sense which it now finds in spiritual things; for those impurities are commonly said to proceed generally from the sweetness which flowed occasionally from the spirit into the sense.

3. The imperfections of the fourth sin, spiritual gluttony, from which the soul is delivered in the dark night, have been discussed in a former chapter, though not all, because they cannot be numbered. Nor shall I speak of them here, for I wish to conclude the subject of this night, that I may pass on to the other, with regard to which I have serious things to write. Let it suffice for a knowledge of the innumerable advantages which the soul, in addition to those already mentioned, gains, in this night, wherewith to resist spiritual gluttony, to say that it is set free from the imperfections there enumerated, and from many other and greater evils than those described, into which many fall, as we learn by experience, because they have not corrected their desires in the matter of spiritual gluttony.

4. For when God has brought the soul into this arid and dark night, He so curbs desire and bridles concupiscence that it can scarcely feed at all upon the sensible sweetness of heavenly or of earthly things, and this so continuously that it corrects, re-forms, and redresses its concupiscence and desires, so that the forces of its passions and concupiscence seem to be destroyed; for as the breast when not given to the babe dries up and withers, so the appetites when not fed upon waste away. Marvellous benefits flow from that spiritual soberness, in addition to those I have mentioned; for because it mortifies concupiscence and desire, the soul dwells in spiritual tranquillity and peace; for, where concupiscence and desire

have no sway, there is no trouble, but, rather, the peace and consolation of God.

5. Another benefit comes from this; a constant remembrance of God, with the fear and dread that it is, as I have said, going back on the spiritual way. This is a great benefit, and not one of the least, of aridity and purgation of the appetite, for the soul is purified and cleansed thereby, from those imperfections which clung to it because of the affections and desires, the effect of which is to darken and deaden the soul.

6. Another very great benefit to the soul in this night is, that it practises many virtues at once, as patience and longsuffering, which are well tried in these aridities, the soul persevering in its spiritual exercises without sweetness or comfort. The love of God is practised, because it is no longer attracted by sweetness and consolation, but by God only. The virtue of fortitude also is practised, because amid these difficulties, and the absence of sweetness in good works from which the soul now suffers, it gathers strength from weakness, and so becomes strong: finally, all the virtues, theological, cardinal, and moral, both in spiritual and corporal matters, are practised amidst these aridities.

7. In this night the soul obtains these four benefits here mentioned, namely, delight of peace, constant remembrance of God, purity and cleanness of soul, the practice of all the virtues of which I have just spoken. So David speaks from his own experience when he was in this night. 'My soul,' he saith, 'refuses to be comforted; I was mindful of God and was delighted, and was exercised, and my spirit fainted.' He adds forthwith: 'I meditated in the night with my own heart, and I was exercised, and I swept my spirit' clean of all affections.

8. The soul is purified also in this aridity of the desires from the imperfections of the other three capital sins of which I have spoken, envy, anger, and sloth, and acquires the opposite virtues. Softened and humbled by these aridities, by the hardships, temptations, and afflictions which in this night try it, it becomes gentle with God, with itself, and with its neighbour. It is no longer impatiently angry

with itself because of its own faults, nor with its neighbour because of his; neither is it discontented or given to unseemly complaints against God because He does not sanctify it at once. As to envy, the soul is in charity with every one, and if any envy remain, it is no longer vicious as before, when the soul was afflicted when it saw others preferred to it, and raised higher; for now it yields to every one considering its own misery, and the envy it feels, if it feels any, is a virtuous envy, a desire to emulate them, which is great virtue.

9. The sloth and weariness now felt in spiritual things are no longer vicious as they were once. They were once the fruit of spiritual delights which the soul experienced at times, and sought after when it had them not. But this present weariness proceeds not from the failure of sweetness, for God has taken it all away in this purgation of the desire.

10. Other innumerable benefits beside these flow from this arid contemplation; for, in the midst of these aridities and hardship, God communicates to the soul, when it least expects it, spiritual sweetness, most pure love, and spiritual knowledge of the most exalted kind, of greater worth and profit than any of which it had previous experience, though at first the soul may not think so, for the spiritual influence now communicated is most delicate, and imperceptible by sense.

11. Finally, as the soul is purified from all sensual affections and desires, it attains to liberty of spirit, wherein the twelve fruits of the Holy Ghost are had. It is also delivered in a most wonderful way from the hands of its three enemies – the devil, the world, and the flesh; for when all the delight and sweetness of sense are quenched, the devil, the world, and the flesh have no weapons and no strength wherewith to assail it.

12. These aridities, then, make the soul love God in all pureness, for now it is influenced not by the pleasure and sweetness which it found in its works – as perhaps it was when that sweetness was present – but by the sole desire to please God. It is not presumptuous and self-satisfied, as perhaps it may have been in the day of its prosperity, but timid and diffident, without any self-satisfaction.

Herein consists that holy fear by which virtues are preserved and grow. This aridity quenches concupiscence, and our natural spirits, as I said before; for now, when God infuses, from time to time, His own sweetness into the soul, it would be strange if it found by any efforts of its own, as has been already said, any comfort or sweetness in any spiritual act or practice.

13. The fear of God and the desire to please Him increase in this arid night; for as the breasts of sensuality, which nourished and sustained the desires which the soul followed after, become dry, nothing remains in that aridity and detachment but an anxious desire to serve God, which is most pleasing unto Him, as it is written: 'a sacrifice to God is an afflicted spirit.'

14. When the soul beholds the many and great benefits which have fallen to its lot in this arid purgation through which it passed, it cries out with truth, 'Oh, happy lot, forth unobserved I went.' I escaped from the bondage and thraldom of my sensual desires and affections, unobserved, so that none of my three enemies were able to hinder me. These enemies of the soul already spoken of so bind and imprison it in sensual desires and affections that it cannot go forth out of itself to the liberty of the perfect love of God; without them they cannot attack it.

15. Hence, when by continual mortification the four passions of the soul are calmed, that is, joy, grief, hope, and fear, when the natural desires are lulled to sleep in our sensual nature by persistent aridities, when the senses and the interior powers of the soul cease to be active, and meditation no longer pursued, as has been already said, which is the household of the lower part of the soul, then the liberty of the spirit is unassailable by these enemies and the house remains calm and tranquil as the words that follow show.

CHAPTER XIV

The last line of the first stanza explained

1. The 'house at rest'.
2. Trials of the night of sense: the sting of the flesh.
3. The spirit of blasphemy.
4. The spirit of giddiness.
5. The soul purified for the divine union by suffering.
6. Duration and intensity of trials determined by God.
7. And proportioned to the strength of the soul.
8. 'To suffer and to be despised.'

'My house being now at rest.' When the house of sensuality was at rest, that is, when the passions were mortified, concupiscence quenched, the desires subdued and lulled to sleep in the blessed night of the purgation of sense, the soul began to set out on the way of the spirit, the way of beginners and proficients, which is also called the illuminative way, or the way of infused contemplation, wherein God Himself teaches and refreshes the soul without meditation or any active efforts that itself may deliberately make. Such, as I have said, is this night and purgation of the senses.

2. But this night, in their case who are to enter into that other more awful night of the spirit, that they may go forward to the divine union of the love of God – it is not every one, but only a few who do so in general – is attended with heavy trials and temptations of sense of long continuance, in some longer than in others; for to some is sent the angel of Satan, the spirit of impurity, to buffet them with horrible and violent temptations of the flesh, to trouble their minds

with filthy thoughts, and their imaginations with representations of sin most vividly depicted; which, at times, becomes an affliction more grievous than death.

3. At other times this night is attended by the spirit of blasphemy; the thoughts and conceptions are overrun with intolerable blasphemies, which now and then are suggested to the imagination with such violence as almost to break forth in words; this, too, is a heavy affliction.

4. Again, another hateful spirit, called by the prophet 'the spirit of giddiness', is suffered to torment them, not that they may fall but as a trial. This spirit so clouds their judgment that they are filled with a thousand scruples and perplexities so embarrassing that they can never satisfy themselves about them, nor submit their judgment therein to the counsel and direction of others. This is one of the most grievous stings and horrors of this night, approaching very nearly to that which takes place in the night of the spirit.

5. God ordinarily sends these violent storms and temptations in the night of the purgation of the sense to those whom he is about to lead afterwards into the other night – though all do not enter in – that being thus chastened and buffeted they may prove themselves, dispose and inure sense and faculties for the union of the divine wisdom to which they are to be then admitted. For if the soul be not tempted, tried, and proved in temptations and afflictions, sense will never attain to wisdom. That is why it is said in Ecclesiasticus, 'What doth he know,' asks the wise man, 'that hath not been tried? . . . he that hath no experience knoweth little . . . he that hath not been tried, what manner of things doth he know?' Jeremias also bears witness to the same truth, saying: 'Thou hast chastised me, and I was instructed.' The most proper form of this chastening, for him who will apply himself unto wisdom, are those interior trials of which I am now speaking. They are that which most effectually purges sense of all sweetness and consolations, to which, by reason of our natural weakness, we are addicted, and by them the soul is really humbled that it may be prepared for its coming exaltation.

6. But how long the soul will continue in this fast and penance of sense, cannot with certainty be told, because it is not the same in all, neither are all subjected to the same temptations. These trials are measured by the divine will, and are proportioned to the imperfections, many or few, to be purged away: and also to the degree of union in love to which God intends to raise the soul: that is the measure of its humiliations, both in their intensity and duration.

7. Those who are strong and more able to bear suffering, are purified in more intense trials, and in less time. But those who are weak are purified very slowly, with weak temptations, and the night of their purgation is long: their senses are refreshed from time to time lest they should fall away; these, however, come late to the pureness of their perfection in this life, and some of them never. These persons are not clearly in the purgative night, nor clearly out of it; for though they make no progress, yet in order that they may be humble and know themselves, God tries them for a season in aridities and temptations, and visits them with His consolations at intervals lest they should become faint-hearted, and seek for comfort in the ways of the world.

8. From other souls, still weaker, God, as it were, hides Himself, that He may try them in His love, for without this hiding of His face from them they would never learn how to approach Him. But those souls that are to enter so blessed and high a state as this of the union of love, however quickly God may lead them, tarry long, in general, amidst aridities and temptations, as we see by experience. But it is now time to begin the explanation of the second night.

BOOK II

OF THE NIGHT OF THE SPIRIT

CHAPTER I

The Second Night; that of the spirit. When it begins

1. Description of a soul which has passed through the sensitive night.
2. Continuation.
3. Continuation.
4. Cause of ecstasies.

The soul, which God is leading onwards, enters not into the night of the spirit at once when it has passed through the aridities and trials of the first purgation and night of sense; yea, rather it must spend some time, perhaps years, after quitting the state of beginners, in exercising itself in the state of proficients. In this state – as one released from a rigorous imprisonment – it occupies itself in divine things with much greater freedom and satisfaction, and its joy is more abundant and interior than it was in the beginning before it entered the night of sense; its imagination and faculties are not held, as hitherto, in the bonds of meditation and spiritual reflections; it now rises at once to most tranquil and loving contemplation, and finds spiritual sweetness without the fatigue of meditation.

2. However, as the purgation of the soul is still somewhat incomplete – the chief part, the purgation of the spirit, being wanting, without which, by reason of the union of our higher and lower nature, man being an individual, the purgation of sense, however violent it may have been, is not finished and perfect – the soul will never be free from some trouble, aridities, darkness, and trials, sometimes much more severe than in the past, which are, as it were, signs and heralds of

the coming night of the spirit, though not so lasting as that expected night; for when the days or the season of this tempestuous night have passed, the soul recovers at once its wonted serenity. It is in this way that God purifies some souls who are not to rise to so high a degree of love as others. He admits them at intervals into the night of contemplation or spiritual purgation, causing the sun to shine upon them, and then to hide its face, according to the words of the Psalmist: 'He sendeth His crystal,' that is contemplation, 'like morsels.' These morsels of dim contemplation are, however, never so intense as is that awful night of contemplation of which I am speaking, and in which God purposely places the soul, that He may raise it to the divine union.

3. That sweetness and interior delight, which proficients find so easily and so plentifully, come now in greater abundance than before, overflowing into the senses more than they were wont to do previous to the purgation of sense. The senses now being more pure, can taste of the sweetness of the spirit in their way with greater ease. But as the sensual part of the soul is weak, without any capacity for the strong things of the spirit, they who are in the state of proficients by reason of the spiritual communications made to the sensual part, are subject therein to great infirmities and sufferings, and physical derangements, and consequently weariness of mind, as it is written: 'the corruptible body . . . presseth down the mind.' Hence the communications made to these cannot be very strong, intense, or spiritual, such as they are required to be for the divine union with God, because of the weakness and corruption of the sensual part which has a share in them.

4. Here is the source of ecstasies, raptures, and dislocation of the bones which always happen whenever these communications are not purely spiritual; that is, granted to the mind alone, as in the case of the perfect, already purified in the second night of the spirit. In these, raptures and physical sufferings have no place, for they enjoy liberty of spirit with unclouded and unsuspended senses. To make it clear how necessary it is for proficients to enter into the night of the spirit, I will now proceed to point out certain imperfections and dangers which beset them.

Chapter II

Of certain imperfections of proficients

1. Habitual imperfections of proficients; roots of sin.
2. Dullness of mind.
3. Actual imperfections of proficients: self–deception.
4. Pride and presumption.
5. Necessity of spiritual night for perfection.
6. Continuation.

Proficients labour under two kinds of imperfections; one habitual, the other actual. The habitual imperfections are their affections and imperfect habits which still remain, like roots, in the mind, where the purgation of sense could not penetrate. The difference between the purgation of these and of the others, is like the difference between plucking out a root, and tearing off a branch; or removing a fresh, and an old stain. For, as I have said, the purgation of sense is, for the spirit, merely the gate and entrance of contemplation, and serves rather to bend sense to the spirit than to unite the latter with God. The stains of the old man still remain in the spirit, though not visible to it, and if they be not removed by the strong soap and lye of the purgation of this night, the spirit cannot attain to the pureness of the divine union.

2. They suffer also from dullness of mind, and natural rudeness which every man contracts by sin; from distraction and dissipation of mind, which must be refined, enlightened, and made recollected in the sufferings and hardships of this night. All those who have not advanced beyond the state of proficients are subject to these habitual

imperfections, which cannot co-exist, as I said before, with the perfect state of union with God in love.

3. But all are not subject to actual imperfections in the same way; some, whose spiritual good is so much on the surface, and so much under the influence of sense, fall into greater unseemlinesses and dangers, of which I spoke in the beginning of this book. For as their mind and sense and feelings are full of fancies whereby they very often see imaginary and spiritual visions – all this, together with other pleasurable impressions, befall many of them in this state, wherein the devil and their own proper fancy most frequently delude the soul – and as Satan is wont with so much sweetness to insinuate, and impress these imaginations, they are easily deluded and influenced by him, because they do not take the precaution to resign themselves into the hands of God, and defend themselves vigorously by faith against these visions and impressions. For now the devil causes many both to believe in vain visions and false prophecies, and to presume that God and His saints are speaking to them: they also frequently believe in their own fancies.

4. Now, too, Satan is wont to fill them with pride and presumption; and they, led on by vanity and arrogance, make a show of themselves in the performance of exterior acts which have an air of sanctity, such as ecstasies and other appearances. They thus become bold with God, losing holy fear, which is the key and guard of all virtue. Some of them become so entangled in manifold falsehoods and delusions, and so persist in them, that their return to the pure road of virtue and real spirituality is exceedingly doubtful. They fall into this miserable condition because they gave way to these spiritual imaginations and feelings with overmuch confidence when they began to advance on the road of spirituality.

5. I have much to say of these imperfections of theirs, and how much more incurable these are than the others, because they consider them as more spiritual than those; but I shall pass on. One thing, however, I must say, to establish the necessity of the spiritual night which is the purgation of the soul that is to go on to perfection, that there is not one among the proficient, however great may be his

exertions, who can be free from many of these natural affections and imperfect habits, the purification of which must, as I have said, necessarily precede the divine union.

6. Besides, and I have said it before, because the spiritual communications reach also to the lower part of the soul, they cannot be as intense, pure, and strong, as the divine union demands, and, therefore, if that is to be attained, the soul must enter the second night of the spirit where – perfectly detaching sense and spirit from all sweetness and from all imaginations – it will travel on the road of faith dark and pure, the proper and adequate means of union, as it is written: 'I will espouse thee to Me in faith,' that is, I will unite Myself to thee in faith.

CHAPTER III

Notes on that which is to follow

1. True spiritual sweetness harmonizes sense with spirit and gives courage to the will.
2. The sensitive night a re-formation of the appetite; the spiritual night a purgation of sense and spirit together.
3. Necessity of courage.
4. Means of the final purification of the soul.
5. Continuation.

Proficients, then, experienced during the past time these sweet communications, in order that the sensual part of the soul, allured and attracted by the spiritual sweetness overflowing from the spirit, may be united and made one with the spiritual part; both parts eating the same spiritual food, each in its own way, off the same dish of their one being, that, thus in a certain way become one and concordant, they might be prepared for the sufferings of the sharp and rough purgation of the spirit which is before them. In that purgation the two parts of the soul, the spiritual and the sensual, are to be wholly purified, for neither of them can be perfectly purified without the other, and the purgation of sense is then effectual when that of the spirit commences in earnest.

2. Hence it is that the night of sense may and should be called a certain re-formation and bridling of desire, rather than purgation, because all the imperfections and disorders of the sensual part having their strength and roots in the mind, the seat of good and evil

"

habits, can never be wholly purged away until the latter, with the rebelliousness and perverseness of the mind, are corrected. Therefore, in this night ensuing, both parts of the soul are purified together: this is the end for which it was necessary to have passed through the re-formation of the first night, and to have attained to that tranquillity which is its fruit, in order that sense and spirit, made one, may both be purified and suffer together with the greater courage, most necessary for so violent and sharp a purgation. For if the weakness of the lower part be not redressed, and if it have acquired no courage in God, in the sweet communions with Him subsequently enjoyed, nature would have been unprepared and without strength for the trials of this night.

3. The intercourse of proficients with God is, however, still most mean, because the gold of the spirit is not purified and refined. They think, therefore, and speak of Him as children, and their feelings are those of children, as described by the Apostle: 'When I was a child, I spake as a child, I understood as a child, I thought as a child'; because they have not reached perfection, which is union with God in love. But in the state of union, having grown to manhood, they do great things in spirit – all their actions and all their faculties being now rather divine than human, as I shall hereafter explain – for God is stripping them of the old man, and clothing them with the new, as it is written: 'Put on the new man, who is created according to God'; and again, 'Be reformed in the newness of your mind.'

4. He now denudes the faculties, the affections, and feelings, spiritual and sensual, interior and exterior, leaving the understanding in darkness, the will dry, the memory empty, the affections of the soul in the deepest affliction, bitterness, and distress; withholding from it the former sweetness it had in spiritual things, in order that this privation may be one of the principles, of which the mind has need, that the spiritual form of the spirit, which is the union of love, may enter into it and be one with it.

5. All this our Lord effects in the soul by means of contemplation, pure and dark, as it is described by it in the first stanza. This stanza,

though explained in reference to the night of sense, the soul under-stands it principally of this second night of the spirit, because that is the chief part of the purification of the soul. I shall, therefore, apply it in this sense, and explain it here again.

CHAPTER IV

Explanation of the first stanza

1. Paraphrase of the first stanza according to the second night.
2. Transformation of the memory, intellect, and will.
3. Continuation.

> *In a dark night,*
> *With anxious love inflamed,*
> *O, happy lot!*
> *Forth unobserved I went,*
> *My house being now at rest.*

Taking these words, then, with reference to purgation, contemplation, or detachment, or poverty of spirit – these are, as it were, one and the same thing – they may be thus explained in this way, as if the soul were saying: In poverty, without protection and help in all my powers, the understanding in darkness, the will under constraint, the memory in trouble and distress, in the dark, in pure faith, which is the dark night of the natural faculties, the will alone touched by grief and affliction, and the anxieties of the love of God, I went forth out of myself, out of my low conceptions and lukewarm love, out of my scanty and poor sense of God, without being hindered by the flesh or the devil.

2. This was to me a great blessing, a happy lot, for by annihilating and subduing my faculties, passions, appetites, and affections – the instruments of my low conceptions of God -- I went forth out of the

scanty works and ways of my own to those of God; that is, my understanding went forth out of itself, and from human and natural became divine; for united to God in that purgation, it understands no more by its natural powers, but in the divine wisdom to which it is united.

3. My will went forth out of itself becoming divine, for now, united with the divine love, it loves no more meanly with the powers of its nature, but with the energy and pureness of the divine spirit. Thus the will acts now in the things of God, not in a human way, and the memory also is transformed in eternal apprehensions of glory. Finally, all the energies and affections of the soul are, in this night and purgation of the old man, renewed into a divine temper and delight.

CHAPTER V

Explains how this dim contemplation is not a night only, but pain and torment also for the soul

1. Definition of the night of the spirit. The will passive save to consent and attend.
2. Why is the divine illumination called night.
3. It is dark to imperfect faculties from excess of light.
4. Dionysius the Areopagite.
5. It is painful from the meeting of contraries.
6. First pain: darkness of self revealed in the light of God.
7. Fear of unworthiness.
8. Second pain: weakness of self felt under the strength of God.
9. To the weak soul the gentle hand of God feels heavy.

In a dark night,

The dark night is a certain inflowing of God into the soul which cleanses it of its ignorances and imperfections, habitual, natural, and spiritual. Contemplatives call it infused contemplation, or mystical theology, whereby God secretly teaches the soul and instructs it in the perfection of love, without efforts on its own part (beyond a loving attention to God, listening to His voice and admitting the light He sends, but without understanding how this is infused contemplation). And inasmuch as it is the loving wisdom of God, it produces special effects in the soul, for it prepares it, by purifying and enlightening it, for union with God in love: it is the same loving wisdom, which by enlightening purifies the blessed spirits, that here purifies and enlightens the soul.

2. But it may be asked: Why does the soul call the divine light, which enlightens the soul and purges it of its ignorances, the dark night? I reply, that the divine wisdom is, for two reasons, not night and darkness only, but pain and torment also to the soul. The first is, the divine wisdom is so high that it transcends the capacity of the soul, and therefore is, in that respect, darkness. The second reason is based on the meanness and impurity of the soul, and in that respect the divine wisdom is painful to it, afflictive and dark also.

3. To prove the truth of the first reason, we take for granted a principle of the philosopher, namely, the more clear and evident divine things are, the more dark and hidden they are to the soul naturally. Thus the more clear the light the more does it blind the eyes of the owl, and the stronger the sun's rays the more it blinds the visual organs; overcoming them, by reason of their weakness, and depriving them of the power of seeing. So the divine light of contemplation, when it beats on the soul, not yet perfectly enlightened, causes spiritual darkness, because it not only surpasses its strength, but because it blinds it and deprives it of its natural perceptions.

4. It is for this reason that St Dionysius and other mystic theologians call infused contemplation a ray of darkness, that is, for the unenlightened and unpurified soul, because this great supernatural light masters the natural power of the reason and takes away its natural way of understanding. Therefore, David also said: 'Cloud and darkness are round about Him;' not that this is so in reality, but in reference to our weak understanding, which, in light so great, becomes dimmed and blind, unable to ascend so high. He repeats it, saying: 'At the brightness that was before Him the clouds passed,' that is, between Him and our understanding. This is the reason why the illuminating ray of hidden wisdom, when God sends it from Himself into the soul not yet transformed, produces thick darkness in the understanding.

5. This dim contemplation is in its beginnings painful also to the soul. For as the infused divine contemplation contains many

excellences in the highest degree, and the soul, which is the recipient, because not yet pure, is involved in many miseries – in the highest degree, too – the result is – as two contraries cannot co-exist in the same subject – that the soul must suffer and be in pain, being the subject in which the two contraries meet, and resist each other because of the purgation of the soul from its imperfections, which is being wrought by contemplation. I shall show it to be so by the following induction.

6. In the first place, because the light and wisdom of contemplation is most pure and bright, and because the soul, on which it beats, is in darkness and impure, that soul which is the recipient must greatly suffer. As eyes weakened and clouded by humours suffer pain when the clear light beats upon them, so the soul, by reason of its impurity, suffers exceedingly when the divine light really shines upon it. And when the rays of this pure light strike upon the soul, in order to expel its impurities, the soul perceives itself to be so unclean and miserable that it seems as if God had set Himself against it, and itself were set against God. So grievous and painful is this feeling – for it thinks now that God has abandoned it – that it was one of the heaviest afflictions of Job during his trial. 'Why hast Thou set me contrary to Thee, and I become burdensome to myself?' The soul seeing distinctly in this bright and pure light, though dimly, its own impurity, acknowledges its own unworthiness before God and all creatures.

7. That which pains it still more is the fear it has that it never will be worthy, and that all its goodness is gone. This is the fruit of that deep impression, made on the mind, in the knowledge and sense of its own wickedness and misery. For now the divine and dim light reveals to it all its wretchedness, and it sees clearly that of itself it can never be other than it is. In this sense we can understand the words of the Psalmist: 'For iniquities Thou hast chastised man, and Thou hast made his soul pine away and wither as a spider.'

8. In the second place, the pain of the soul comes from its natural, moral, and spiritual weakness; for when this divine

contemplation strikes it with a certain vehemence, in order to strengthen it and subdue it, it is then so pained in its weakness as almost to faint away, particularly at times when the divine contemplation strikes it with greater vehemence; for sense and spirit, as if under a heavy and gloomy burden, suffer and groan in agony so great that death itself would be a desired relief.

9. This was the experience of Job, and he said, 'I will not that He contend with me with much strength, nor that He oppress me with the weight of His greatness.' The soul under the burden of this oppression feels itself so removed out of God's favour that it thinks – and so it is – that all things which consoled it formerly have utterly failed it, and that no one is left to pity it. Job also speaks to the same purport, 'Have mercy upon me, have mercy upon me, at the least you my friends, because the hand of our Lord hath touched me.' Wonderful and piteous sight! So great are the weakness and impurity of the soul that the hand of God, so soft and so gentle, is felt to be so heavy and oppressive, though neither pressing nor resting on it, but merely touching it, and that, too, most mercifully; for He touches the soul not to chastise it, but to load it with His graces.

Chapter VI

Of other sufferings of the soul in this night

1. Third pain: loss of God felt in conscious unworthiness.
2. The soul feels abandoned by God and man.
3. Continuation.
4. Jonas.
5. Fourth pain: emptiness of self felt in the fullness of God.
6. Continuation.
7. Spiritual suffocation.
8. Illustrations from Holy Scripture.
9. Continuation.
10. Purgatory in this life.

The third kind of suffering and pain for the soul comes from the meeting of two extremes, the human and the divine: the latter is the purgative contemplation; the human is the soul itself. The divine touches the soul to renew it and to ripen it, in order to make it divine, to detach it from the habitual affections and qualities of the old man, to which it clings and conforms itself. The divine extreme so breaks and bruises the spiritual substance, swallowing it up in profound darkness, that the soul, at the sight of its own wretchedness, seems to perish and waste away, by a cruel spiritual death, as if it were swallowed up and devoured by a wild beast, suffering the pangs of Jonas in the belly of the whale. For it must lie buried in the grave of a gloomy death that it may attain to the spiritual resurrection for which it hopes. David describes this kind of pain and suffering – though it really baffles description – when he says, 'The sorrows of death have compassed me . . . the sorrows of hell have compassed me . . . In my tribulation I have called upon our Lord, and have cried to my God.'

2. But the greatest affliction of the sorrowful soul in this state is the thought that God has abandoned it, of which it has no doubt; that He has cast it away into darkness as an abominable thing. The thought that He has abandoned it is a grievous and pitiable affliction. David experienced the same trials when he said, 'As the wounded sleeping in the sepulchres, of whom Thou art mindful no more; and they are cast off from Thy hand. They have put me in the lower lake, in the dark places, and in the shadow of death. Thy fury is confirmed upon me; and all Thy waves Thou hast brought in upon me.'

3. For, in truth, when the soul is in the pangs of the purgative contemplation, the shadow of death and the pains and torments of hell are most acutely felt, that is, the sense of being without God, being chastised and abandoned in His wrath and heavy displeasure. All this and even more the soul feels now, for a fearful apprehension has come upon it that thus it will be with it for ever. It has also the same sense of abandonment with respect to all creatures, and that it is an object of contempt to all, especially to its friends; and so the Psalmist continues, saying, 'Thou hast put away my acquaintance far from me; they have set me an abomination to themselves.'

4. The prophet Jonas also, as one who had experience of this, both bodily in the belly of the whale and spiritually, witnesses to the same truth, saying, 'Thou hast cast me forth into the depth, in the heart of the sea, and a flood hath compassed me: all Thy surges and Thy waves have passed over me. And I said, I am cast away from the sight of Thine eyes: but yet I shall see Thy holy temple again,' – this is the purgation of the soul that it may see God – 'the waters have compassed me even to the soul, the depth hath enclosed me, the sea hath covered my head. I am descended to the extreme parts of the mountains: the bars of the earth have shut me up for ever.' The bars

of the earth here are the imperfections of the soul which hinder it from having any joy in this sweet contemplation.

5. The fourth kind of pain is caused by another excellence peculiar to this dim contemplation, a sense of its majesty and greatness, which makes the soul conscious of the other extreme, its own poverty and misery; this is one of the chief sufferings of this purgation. The soul is conscious of a profound emptiness, and destitution of the three kinds of goods, natural, temporal, and spiritual, which are ordained for its comfort; it sees itself in the midst of the opposite evils, miserable imperfections and aridities, emptiness of the understanding, and abandonment of the spirit in darkness.

6. Inasmuch as God is now purifying the soul in its sensual and spiritual substance, its interior and exterior powers, it is necessary for it that it should be in all its relations empty, poor, and abandoned, in aridity, emptiness, and darkness. For the sensual part is purified in aridities, the faculties in the emptiness of their powers, and the spirit in the thick darkness.

7. All this God brings about by means of this dim contemplation, in which the soul is made to suffer from the failure and withdrawal of its natural powers, which is a most distressing pain. It is like that of a person being suffocated, or hindered from breathing. But this contemplation is also purifying the soul, undoing or emptying it, or consuming in it, as fire consumes the rust and mouldiness of the metal, all the affections and habits of imperfection which it had contracted in the whole course of its life. But inasmuch as these habits are deeply rooted in the substance of the soul, the grievous interior sufferings and trials it has to undergo are heavy, and are, in addition to the destitution and emptiness, natural and spiritual, of which I have spoken.

8. The words of the prophet Ezechiel are now fulfilled: 'Heap together the bones which I will burn with fire: the flesh shall be consumed, and the whole composition shall be sodden, and the bones shall dry away.' This describes the pain which the soul suffers in the sensual and spiritual parts when in this state of emptiness and poverty. Then the prophet proceeds, saying: 'Set it also upon hot

burning coals empty, that the brass thereof may wax hot and be melted; and let the filth of it be melted in the midst thereof, and let the rust thereof be consumed.'

9. This is the heavy trial of the soul in the purifying fires of contemplation. The prophet says that, in order to purge away and consume the filth of the affections which are within the soul, it is necessary for it in a certain way to be annihilated and undone, because its passions and affections have become natural to it. The soul, therefore, because it is purified in this furnace, like gold in a crucible, according to the words of Wisdom, 'as gold in the furnace He hath proved them' feels itself utterly consumed in its innermost substance in this absolute poverty wherein it is as it were lost. This is taught us by the Psalmist, saying of himself: 'Save me, O God, because waters are entered unto my soul. I stick fast in the mire of the depth; and there is no sure standing. I am come into the depth of the sea; and a tempest hath overwhelmed me. I have laboured crying, my jaws are made hoarse, my eyes have failed, whilst I hope in my God.'

10. Here God is humbling the soul that He may exalt it much hereafter, and if it were not His will that these feelings, when they rise, should be quickly lulled again, the soul would almost immediately depart from the body, but they occur only at intervals in their greatest violence. They are occasionally felt so acutely that the soul seems to see hell and perdition open before it. Of these, are they who go down alive into hell, and have their purgatory in this life; for this is the purgation to be endured there. And thus the soul which passes through this state in the present life, either enters not into purgatory, or is detained there but a moment, for one hour here is of greater profit than many there.

CHAPTER VII

The same subject continued. Other afflictions and trials of the will

1. Fifth pain: the memory of past happiness. Job.
2. Jeremias.
3. The suffering soul worthy of compassion.
4. It derives no relief from spiritual advice.
5. God the only consolation.
6. Duration and intermission of spiritual sufferings.
7. One intense emotion excludes its contrary.
8. The soul still conscious of imperfections and of danger.
9. Vicissitudes of joy and of sorrow.
10. The pain increased.

The afflictions and distress of the will now are also very great; they occasionally pierce the soul with a sudden recollection of the evils that environ it, and of the uncertainty of relief. To this is superadded the memory of past happiness; for they who enter this night have, generally, had much sweetness in God, and served Him greatly; but now, to see themselves strangers to so much happiness, and unable to recover it, causes them the greatest affliction.

2. Job also, having learnt this by experience, declares it in these words: 'I, sometime that wealthy one, suddenly am broken; He hath held my neck, broken me, and set me to himself, as it were a mark. He hath compassed me with His spears, He hath wounded my loins, He hath not spared, and hath poured out on the earth my bowels. He

hath cut me with wound upon wound: He hath come violently upon me as it were a giant. I have sewed sackcloth upon my skin, and have covered my flesh with ashes. My face is swollen with weeping, and my eyelids are dim.' So many and so great are the torments of this night, and so many the places in the Holy Writings, which may be quoted to this effect, that time and strength would fail me were I to enumerate them. For no doubt, all that can be said will fall short; something may be gathered on the matter from the texts already before us.

2. And now to conclude the subject of the first line of the stanza, and to show yet a little more what this night is to the soul, I will repeat how it was felt by the prophet Jeremias, who, great though he was, bewailed it in many words, saying thus: 'I, the man that see my poverty in the rod of His indignation. He hath led me and brought me into darkness, and not into light. Only against me He hath turned, and hath converted His hand all the day. He hath made my skin old and my flesh; He hath broken my bones. He hath built round about me, and He hath compassed me with gall and labour. In dark places He hath placed me as the everlasting dead. He hath built round about against me, I go not forth. He hath aggravated my fetters. Yea, and when I shall cry and ask, He hath excluded my prayer. He hath shut up my ways with square stones. He hath subverted my paths. He is become unto me a bear lying in wait; a lion in secret places. He hath subverted my paths, and hath broken me; He hath made me desolate. He hath bent His bow, and set me as a mark for the arrow. He hath shot in my reins the daughters of His quiver. I am made a derision to all my people, their song all the day. He hath replenished me with bitterness, He hath inebriated me with wormwood. And He hath broken my teeth by number; He hath fed me with ashes. And my soul is repelled from peace; I have forgotten good things. And I said: Mine end is perished and mine hope from our Lord. Remember my poverty and transgression, the wormwood and the gall. Remembering I will be mindful; and my soul shall languish in me.'

3. These are the lamentations of the prophet over these pains and

trials, whereby he most vividly depicts the sufferings of the soul, which come upon it in this purgation and spiritual night. That soul is worthy of all compassion which God leads into this dreadful and horrible night. For, although it is well with it because of the great blessing of which this night is the source, for, as Job saith, God will raise up good things for it out of this darkness, and bring light over the shadow of death: 'Who revealeth profound things out of darkness, and bringeth forth the shadow of death into light'; so that his light shall be as the darkness; 'the darkness thereof so also the light thereof,' as David speaks. Nevertheless, because of the excessive pain it endures, and the great uncertainty of relief, it imagines now, as the prophet says, that its calamities will never come to an end. God, in the words of David, having made it to 'dwell in darkness as those that have been dead of old,' the spirit being in anguish within it, and 'the heart within' it 'troubled', it is a very painful and pitiable state.

4. Besides, the soul derives no consolation now in the advice that may be given it, or from its spiritual director, because of the loneliness and desolation of this dark night. Though its confessor may set before it in many ways good reasons why it should be comforted because of the blessings which these pains supply, the soul will not believe him. For as it is so filled with and overwhelmed by its sense of these evils, whereby it discerns so clearly its own misery, it imagines that its spiritual director, not seeing that which itself sees and feels, speaks as he does without comprehending its state, and, instead of being comforted, is pained anew, for it considers that his counsel cannot relieve its misery; and in truth so it is, for until our Lord shall have perfected the purification of the soul, according to His will, no help and no remedy can be of any service or profit in this pain.

5. Moreover, the soul can do so little in this state; like a prisoner in a gloomy dungeon, bound hand and foot, it cannot stir, neither can it see or feel any relief, either from above or below, until the spirit is softened, humbled, and purified; until it becomes so refined, simple, and pure, as to become one with the Spirit of God in that degree of the union of love which He in His mercy intends for it, and

corresponding to which is the greater or less violence, the longer or shorter duration, of this purgation.

6. But if this purgation is to be real it will last, notwithstanding its vehemence, for some years, but admitting of intermissions and relief, during which, by the dispensation of God, the dim contemplation divested of its purgative form and character assumes that of the illuminative and of love. Under this form of it, the soul, like one escaped from the dungeons of its prison into the comfort of space and freedom, enjoys the sweetness of peace, and the loving tenderness of God in the flowing abundance of spiritual communications. This is to the soul a sign of the spiritual health which is being wrought within by this purgation, and a foretaste of the abundance it hopes for. So much so is this at times that it thinks all its trials are over. For such is the nature of spiritual things in the soul, when they are most purely spiritual, that the soul thinks when trials return they will never end, and that all its blessings have perished; and when it prospers in its spiritual course it thinks all its calamities are past, and that it shall always abound in good things. Thus it was with David when he said: 'In my abundance I said: I shall never be moved.'

7. The reason of this is that the actual presence of one thing in the mind is naturally inconsistent with the presence and sense of its contrary; this is not so much so in the sensual part of the soul, because of the weakness of its apprehension. But as the spirit is not yet wholly purified and cleansed from the imperfections contracted by its lower nature, though more consistent now, it is liable to further sufferings, so far as it is under the dominion of these affections, as we see in the many afflictions and distress of David after the change, though he had said in the day of his prosperity, 'I shall never be moved.'

8. In the same way the soul, amidst the abundance of spiritual blessings, but not observing the root of imperfection and impurity which still remains, thinks that all its trials are over. This thought, however, is of rare occurrence, for until the spiritual purgation is complete, the sweet communications are rarely so abundant as to conceal the root that remains behind, in such a way that the soul

shall not be inwardly conscious of some deficiency, or that something still is to be done. Nor is the communication such as to allow it to enjoy the relief that is offered it perfectly, for it feels as if an enemy were lurking within, who, though he may be as if subdued and asleep, the soul fears may yet return in his strength and assault it as before.

9. And so it comes to pass, for when the soul is most secure, and least expects it, it returns, drags down the soul, and then plunges it at once into another affliction heavier, darker, and sadder than the previous one, and which, perhaps, will be of longer continuance. The soul again is convinced that all its good is gone from it for ever. Experience cannot teach it: the blessings that followed its former trials, during which it thought that its sufferings would never end, cannot hinder it from believing, during its present trials, that all its good has perished, and that it will never be again with it as it was before. For, as I am saying, this belief, so persistent, is wrought in the soul by the present impression made on the mind, which destroys within it all that is contrary thereto. This is the reason why the souls in purgatory suffer much at the thought they shall never leave that place and their torments shall never cease. For although they possess the three theological virtues, faith, hope, and charity as habits, they derive no benefit or consolation from any acts of these virtues on account of the ever-present sense of their pain and of the privation of God; even if they succeed in seeing how much they love God, yet this is no source of consolation because it is by no means certain to them that God loves them nor that they are worthy of His love; on the contrary, seeing themselves deprived of Him and given over to their misery, they discover good reason within themselves for being abhorred and rejected by Him for ever.

10. Thus the soul in this purgation, though it seems to love God greatly, and is ready to die for Him a thousand deaths – and that is true, for souls thus tried love God with great sincerity, nevertheless they find no relief, but rather an increase of pain herein. For seeking God alone, and naught else, seeing also its own great misery, it cannot believe that God loves it, nor that it is, or ever will be, worthy

of love, but rather is convinced that there is that in it which should make it hated not only of God, but of all creatures also for ever; it grieves to see that of itself it deserves to be abandoned of Him Whom it so loves and so longs for.

Chapter VIII

Of other sufferings which distress the soul in this state

1. Sixth pain: inability to fix the attention on God or divine things.
2. Loss of mental power.
3. Annihilation.
4. Faculties of the soul absorbed in God.
5. The light of reason dim in the light of God.
6. An analogy: natural light perceptible only when reflected by objects.
7. Marks of a purified mind.

Another source of much affliction and distress to the soul in this state is that, as the dark night hinders the exercise of the faculties and affections, it cannot lift up the heart and mind to God as before, nor pray to Him. It thinks itself to be in that state described by Jeremias when he said, 'Thou hast set a cloud before Thee, that prayer may not pass.' This is the meaning of the words quoted before – 'He hath shut up my ways with square stones.' If at any time it prays, it prays with so much aridity, and without sweetness, so as to think that God neither hears nor regards it; as the prophet tells us in the same place, saying, 'Yea, and when I shall cry, and ask, He excludeth my prayer.' And, in truth, this is not the time for the soul to speak to God, but, in the words of Jeremias, to put its 'mouth in the dust', suffering in patience this purgation.

2. It is God Himself Who is now working in the soul, and the soul is therefore powerless. Hence it comes that it cannot pray or give

much attention to divine things. Neither can it attend to temporal matters, for it falls into frequent distractions, and the memory is so profoundly weakened, that many hours pass by without its knowing what it has done or thought, what it is doing or is about to do; nor can it give much heed to what it is occupied with, notwithstanding all its efforts.

3. Inasmuch, then, as not only the understanding is purified from its imperfect perceptions, and the will from its affections, but the memory, also, from all its knowledge and reflections, it is necessary that the soul should be annihilated herein, that the words of the Psalmist, when he was in this purgation, may be fulfilled: 'I am brought to nothing, and I knew not.' This 'knowing not' extends to these follies and failures of the memory. These wanderings and failures of the memory are the result of interior recollection, by which the soul is absorbed in contemplation. For in order to prepare the soul, and temper it divinely in all its powers for the divine union of love, it must, first of all, be absorbed with all its powers in the divine and dim spiritual light of contemplation, and be thus detached from all affection for, and apprehension of, created things. This continues ordinarily in proportion to the intensity of its contemplation.

4. Thus, then, the more pure and simple the divine light when it beats on the soul, the more does it darken it, empty it, and annihilate it, as to all its apprehensions and affections, whether they regard heavenly or earthly things. And also, the less pure and simple the light, the less is the soul darkened and annihilated. It seems strange to say, that the purer and clearer the supernatural and divine light the more is it in the soul, and that it is less so when less pure.

5. But this may be easily explained; if we keep in mind the saying of the philosopher that supernatural things are more dark to the understanding the more clear and evident they are in themselves. A likeness taken from ordinary natural light will make this quite clear. A sunbeam coming in by the window is perceived the less distinctly the more pure and free from atoms and motes the air is, but the more of these there are, the more distinct is the beam to the eye. The reason is that we do not see light itself, but by means of it we see the

objects on which it falls, and these reflecting it, the light itself becomes a visible object; had it not struck them it would itself remain invisible. Thus, if the beam entered by one window, passed through the middle of the room without encountering any object that could reflect it, no atoms nor even air, and went out by a window opposite, the room would not be lit up, neither would the beam be visible. On the contrary, if we think well of it, the line of the beam would be plunged in deeper darkness, for not only would it not be visible but it would absorb what faint light there might be, for as we suppose there are no objects whatever to reflect it. Thus this ray of divine contemplation, transcending as it does the natural powers, striking the soul with its divine light, makes it dark, and deprives it of all the natural affections and apprehensions which it previously entertained in its own natural light. Under these circumstances, the soul is left not only in darkness but in emptiness also, as to its powers and desires, both natural and spiritual, and in this emptiness and darkness is purified and enlightened by the divine spiritual light, but it does not imagine that it has it; yea, rather, it thinks itself to be in darkness, as we have said of the sunbeam which, though passing through the middle of a room, cannot be seen if the air is quite pure and there are no objects on which it may fall.

6. However, the spiritual light falling on the soul if there is anything to reflect it, that is, upon any matter, however small, of perfection, which presents itself to the understanding or a decision to be made as to the truth or falsehood of anything, the soul sees it at once, and understands the matter more clearly than it ever did before it entered into this darkness. In the same way the soul discerns the spiritual light which is given it that it may easily recognize its own imperfection; thus, the ray of light in a room, which we said was of itself not so visible, but when the hand or any other object is held before it, the hand is seen forthwith, and the light of the sun is known to be there.

7. Then, because this spiritual light is so clear, pure, and diffused, neither confined to, nor specially related to, any particular matter of the understanding, natural or divine, seeing that with respect to all

such matters the powers of the soul are empty and as if they did not exist – the soul in great ease and freedom discerns and searches into everything high or low, that is presented to it; and for that reason the Apostle said, 'The Spirit searcheth all things, even the profundities of God'; for it is of this pure and diffused wisdom that we are to understand that which the Holy Ghost spake by the mouth of the wise man, 'Wisdom reacheth everywhere by reason of her clearness;' that is, because not connected with any particular object of the understanding or affection. The characteristic of a mind purified and annihilated as to all particular objects of affection and of the understanding, is to have no pleasure in, or knowledge of, anything in particular; to abide in emptiness and darkness; to embrace all things in its grand comprehensiveness, that it may fulfil mystically the words of the Apostle, 'having nothing and possessing all things,' for such poverty of spirit merits such a blessing.

CHAPTER IX

How this night enlightens the mind, though it brings darkness over it

1. Light, love and liberty found in the night of the spirit. Illustration from the primary elements of matter.
2. One selfish affection or apprehension may make perfection impossible.
3. Because the natural cannot itself reach the supernatural.
4. Purification of grace equal to the habits of nature.
5. Continuation.
6. The soul prepared by suffering for the spirit of God.
7. The soul – an exile in the world – at home in God.
8. Continuation.
9. In the spiritual night false peace is lost, true peace is found.
10. Unsettling.
11. Example of Job.
12. Great works require great labour.
13. Beginning of contemplation painful. Self the cause of suffering.

It remains for me now to explain that this blessed night, though it darkens the mind, does so only to give it light in everything; and though it humbles it and makes it miserable, does so only to raise it up and set it free; and though it impoverishes it and empties it of all its natural self and liking, it does so only to enable it to reach forward divinely to the possession and fruition of all things, both of heaven and earth, in perfect liberty of spirit. As it is fitting that the primary elements, that they may enter into the composition of all natural substances, should have no colour, taste, nor smell peculiar to themselves, in order that they may combine with all colours, all tastes, and all smell, so the mind must be pure, simple, and detached from all kinds of natural affections, actual and habitual, in order that it may be able to participate freely in the largeness of spirit of the divine wisdom, wherein by reason of its pureness it tastes of the sweetness of all things in a certain pre-eminent way. And without this purgation it is altogether impossible to taste of the abundance of these spiritual delights. For one single affection remaining in the soul, or any one matter to which the mind clings either habitually or actually, is sufficient to prevent all perception and all communication of the tender and interior sweetness of the spirit of love, which contains within itself all sweetness supremely.

2. As the children of Israel, merely on account of that single affection for, and remembrance of, the fleshpots of Egypt, could not taste the delicious bread of angels, the manna in the desert, which, as the divine writings tell us, had 'the sweetness of all taste', and 'turned to that every man would', so the mind which is still subject to any actual or habitual affection or particular or narrow mode of apprehending, or understanding anything, cannot taste the sweetness of the spirit of liberty, according to the desire of the will. The reason is this: the affections, feelings, and apprehensions of the perfect spirit, being of so high an order and specially divine, are of another kind and different from those which are natural; and in order to be actually and habitually enjoyed, require the annihilation of the latter, as happens with two contraries which cannot co-exist in the same subject.

3. It is therefore very expedient and necessary, if the soul is to advance to these heights, that the dark night of contemplation should first bring it to nothing, and undo it in all its meannesses, bringing it into darkness, aridities, loneliness, and emptiness; for the light that is to be given it is a certain divine light of the highest

nature, surpassing all natural light, and not naturally cognizable by the understanding. If the understanding is to be united with that light, and become divine in the state of perfection, it must first of all be purified and annihilated as to its natural light, which must be brought actually into darkness by means of this dim contemplation.

4. This darkness must continue so long as it is necessary to destroy the habit, long ago contracted, of understanding things in a natural way, and until the divine enlightening shall have taken its place. And therefore inasmuch as the power of understanding, previously exerted, is natural, the result is that the darkness now endured is awful, and most afflictive, as it were solid, because it reaches to, and is felt in, the innermost depths of the spirit. In the same way, inasmuch as the affection of love, communicated in the divine union, is divine, and therefore most spiritual, subtle, delicate, and most interior, surpassing all sense and affection, natural and imperfect, of the will and every desire of the same, it is necessary for the perception and fruition, in the union of love, of this divine affection and most exquisite delight, that the will, by nature incapable of it, should be first purified and annihilated, as to all its affections and feelings, left in darkness and distress proportional to the intensity of the habit of natural affections it had acquired, in respect both of human and divine things.

5. And this must be done, in order that the will, in the fire of dim contemplation, wasted, withered, and deprived of all selfishness – like the liver of the fish which Tobias laid on the burning coals – may acquire a pure and simple disposition, a purified and sound taste, so as to feel those sublime and wonderful touches of divine love when it shall be divinely transformed; all its former contrarieties actual and habitual being expelled.

6. Moreover, in order to attain to the divine union, for which the dark night disposes it, the soul must be endowed and replenished with a certain glorious magnificence in the divine communication, which includes innumerable blessings and joys, surpassing all the abundance which the soul can naturally possess (it being too weak and impure) – so speak the prophet Isaias and St Paul, 'Eye hath not

seen, nor ear heard, neither hath it entered into the heart of man what things God hath prepared for them that love Him,' it is necessary for it that it should be first brought into a state of emptiness and spiritual poverty, detached from all help and consolation in all the things of heaven and earth, that being thus empty it may be really poor in spirit and divested of the old man, and may live that new and blessed life to which it attains in this dark night which is the state of union with God.

7. And because the soul is to attain to the possession of a certain sense, and divine knowledge, most generous and full of sweetness, of all human and divine things which do not fall within the common-sense and natural perceptions of the soul – it views them with different eyes now; as the light and grace of the Holy Ghost differ from those of sense, the divine from the human – it is necessary that the spirit should be brought low, and inured to hardships in all that relates to the natural and common sense. It must suffer hardships and afflictions in the purgative contemplation, and the memory must become a stranger to all pleasing and peaceful knowledge, with a most interior sense and feeling of being a stranger and a pilgrim here, so that all things shall seem strange to it, and other than they were wont to seem.

8. For this night is drawing the spirit away from its ordinary and common sense of things, that it may draw it towards the divine sense, which is a stranger and an alien to all human ways; so much so that the soul seems to be carried out of itself. At other times it looks upon itself as if under the influence of some charm or spell, and is amazed at all that it hears and sees, which seem to it to be most strange and out of the way, though in reality they are, as they usually are, the same. The reason is this: the soul has become a stranger to the ordinary sense of things, in order that being brought to nothing therein, it might be informed in the divine. Now this belongs more to the next life than to this.

9. The soul suffers all these afflictive purgations of the spirit that it may be born again to the life of the spirit through the divine inflowing, and in these pangs bring forth the spirit of salvation,

fulfilling the words of Isaias: 'So are we become in Thy presence, O Lord. We have conceived, and been as it were in labour, and have brought forth the spirit' of salvation. Moreover, as in the night of contemplation the soul is prepared for that tranquillity and inward peace which is such and so full of delight as, in the words of Scripture, to 'pass all understanding,' it is necessary for the soul that all its former peace, which, because involved in so many imperfections, was no peace, though it seemed to be a twofold peace, namely, of sense and spirit – that is, seeing itself filled with the spiritual treasures of this peace of the senses and of the soul, it, being as yet imperfect, imagined itself as having already acquired this twofold peace) – because it was pleasing, should first of all be purified, and the soul withdrawn from and disturbed in that imperfect peace, as Jeremias felt and lamented in the words cited before to express the trials of the night that is now past, namely: 'My soul is repelled from peace.'

10. This is a painful unsettling, full of misgivings, imaginations, and inward struggles, in which the soul, at the sight and in the consciousness of its own misery, imagines itself to be lost, and all its good to have perished for ever. In this state the spirit is pierced by sorrow so profound as to occasion strong spiritual groans and cries, to which at times it gives utterance, and tears break forth, if there be any strength left for them, though this relief is but rarely granted. The royal prophet David has well described this state, being one who had great experience of it, saying, 'I am afflicted and humbled exceedingly; I roared with the groaning of my heart.' This roaring proceeds from great pain; for sometimes the sudden and sharp recollection of the miseries that environ the soul, makes it rise and surround the affections of the soul with such pain and grief that I know not how it can be explained otherwise than by the words of Job: 'as overflowing waters so is my roaring.' For as waters sometimes overflow, drown and fill all places, so this roaring, and sense of pain, become occasionally so strong as to flow over and into the soul, filling all its deepest affections and energies with spiritual pain and sorrow which defy all exaggeration.

11. Such is the work wrought in the soul by this night that hideth the hopes of the light of day. It was in reference to it that Job said, 'In the night my mouth is pierced with sorrows, and they that feed upon me do not sleep.' The mouth here is the will, pierced by these sorrows which cease not to tear the soul, neither do they sleep, for the doubts and misgivings which harass it are never at rest.

12. This warfare and combat are deep, because the peace hoped for is most deep: the spiritual sorrow is interior, refined, and pure, because the love to be enjoyed must be also most interior and pure. The more interior and perfect the work, the more interior, perfect, and pure must the labour be that produces it; and the stronger the building, the more solid it is. 'My soul fadeth within myself,' saith Job, 'and the days of affliction possess me. So, in the same way, because the soul has to attain to the enjoyment and possession, in the state of perfection to which it journeys in this purgative night, of innumerable blessings, of gifts, and virtues, both in the substance of the soul and in the powers thereof, it is necessary that it should first consider and feel itself generally a stranger to and deprived of them all, empty and poor, and regard them as so far beyond its reach as to be persuaded that it never can attain to them, and that all goodness is perished from it. This is the meaning of those words of Jeremias, 'I have forgotten good things.'

13. Let us now see why the light of contemplations so sweet and lovely to the soul that nothing is more desirable – for it is that, as I said before, whereby the divine union takes place, and whereby the soul in the state of perfection finds all the good it desires – produces, when it strikes the soul, these painful beginnings and terrible effects. The answer is easy, and is already given in part; there is nothing in contemplation and the divine inflowing, to cause pain, but rather much sweetness and joy, as the soul will find later. The cause is the imperfection and weakness of the soul, and dispositions not fit for the reception of this sweetness. And so, when the divine light beats upon the soul, it makes it suffer in the way described.

CHAPTER X

Explanation of this purgation by a comparison

1. Analogy of the action of fire.
2. The divine fire.
3. The same cause purifies and transforms the soul.
4. Weakness and imperfection the source of suffering.
5. Text.
6. Cause of purgatory.
7. Transformation of love equal to purification by suffering.
8. Deeper fire, greater sufferings.
9. Cause of absence of consolation.
10. The soul conscious of remaining imperfections.
11. To die or to suffer.

To make what I have said, and what I have still to say, more clear, it is well to observe here that this purgative and loving knowledge, or divine light, of which I have spoken, is to the soul which it is purifying, in order to unite it perfectly to itself, as fire is to fuel which it is transforming into itself. The first action of material fire on fuel is to dry it, to expel from it all water and all moisture. It blackens it at once and soils it, producing a disagreeable smell, and drying it by little and little, makes it light and consumes all its foulness and blackness which are contrary to itself. Finally, having heated and set on fire its outward surface, it transforms the whole into itself, and makes it beautiful as itself. The fuel under these conditions retains neither active nor passive qualities of its own, except bulk and weight, and assumes all the properties and acts of fire. It becomes dry, being dry it glows, and glowing, burns; luminous, it gives light, and burns more quickly than before. All this is the property and effect of fire.

2. It is in this way we have to reason about the divine fire of contemplative love which, before it unites with, and transforms the soul into, itself, purges away all its contrary qualities. It expels its impurities, blackens it and obscures it, and thus its condition is apparently worse than it was before, more impure and offensive. For while the divine purgation is removing all the evil and vicious humours, which, because so deeply rooted and settled in the soul, were neither seen nor felt, but now, in order to their expulsion and annihilation, are rendered clearly visible in the dim light of the divine contemplation, the soul – though not worse in itself, nor in the sight of God – seeing at last what it never saw before, looks upon itself not only as unworthy of His regard, but even as a loathsome object and that God does loathe it. By this comparison we shall be able to understand much that I have said, and purpose to say.

3. In the first place, we can see how that very light, and that loving knowledge which unites the soul and transforms it into itself, is the same which purifies and prepares it; for the fire that transforms the fuel and incorporates it with itself, is the very same which also at the first prepared it for that end.

4. In the second place, we may see that these sufferings of the soul do not proceed from the divine wisdom – it being written, 'All good things came to me together with her,' – but from its own weakness and imperfection, being incapable, previous to its purgation, of receiving this divine light, sweetness, and delight; and that is the reason why its sufferings are so great. The fuel is not transformed into fire, at the instant of their contact, if it be not previously prepared for burning.

5. This is the experience of the Wise Man, who thus describes his sufferings before his union with, and possession of, wisdom: 'My soul hath wrestled in it . . . My belly was troubled in seeking it; therefore shall I possess a good possession.'

6. In the third place we learn by the way how souls suffer in

purgatory. The fire, though applied, would have no power over them if they had no imperfections for which they must suffer, for these are the matter on which that fire seizes; when that matter is consumed there is nothing more to burn. So is it here, when all imperfections are removed, the suffering of the soul ceases, and in its place comes joy.

7. In the fourth place, we learn that the soul, the more it is purified and cleansed in the fire of love, the more it glows with it. The better the fuel is prepared for the fire the better it burns. The soul, however, is not always conscious of this burning of love within it, but only now and then, when the contemplation is less profound, for the soul is then able to observe, and even to delight in, the work that is being wrought, because it is visible; the hand of the artificer seems to be withdrawn from the work, and the iron taken out of the furnace, so as to show in some measure the work that is being wrought. Then, too, the soul is able to see in itself that good which it did not see while the process was going on. Thus, when the flame ceases to envelop the fuel, it is possible to see clearly how much of it has been burnt.

8. In the fifth place, we shall also find by this comparison that which has been said before, namely, how true it is that after these consolations, the soul suffers again more intensely and keenly than it did before. For after the manifestation of the work that has been done, when the more outward imperfections have been expelled, the fire of love returns again to purge and consume that which is more interior. The suffering of the soul herein becomes more penetrating, deep, and spiritual, according as it refines away the more profound, subtle, and deeply rooted interior imperfections of the spirit. It is here as with the fuel in the fire, the deeper the fire penetrates the greater is its force and energy in disposing the inmost substance of the fuel for its own possession of it.

9. In the sixth place will be seen the reason why the soul believes that all its goodness has been consumed and that it is full of evil, since nothing but bitterness penetrates it at this time; thus neither air nor any other object touches the burning wood, only the fire which consumes it. But at those moments of respite the joy will be

more interior because the purification has gone deeper.

10. In the seventh place, we shall learn that the soul, though it rejoices intensely in these intervals of peace – so much so that it seems at times, as we have said, to think its trials over, never to return, even while it is certain that they will soon return – cannot but feel, if it observes a single root of imperfection behind – and sometimes it must do so – that its joy is not full. It seems as if that root threatened to spring up anew, and when that is so, it does so quickly.

11. Finally, that which still remains to be purified and enlightened within cannot well be concealed from the soul in the presence of that which has been already purified; so also that portion of the fuel which is still to be set on fire is very different from that which the flame has purified. And when this purgation commences anew in the inmost soul, it is not strange that it should consider all its goodness to have perished, and think that it can never recover its former prosperity; for in most interior sufferings all outward goodness is hidden from it.

12. Keeping this comparison, then, before our eyes, with that which I have already said, on the first line of this stanza, concerning this dark night and its fearful characteristics, it may be well to leave the subject of these afflictions of the soul, and to enter on the matter of the fruit of its tears and their blessed properties, of which the soul sings in the second line.

CHAPTER XI

Begins the explanation of the second line of the first stanza, and shows how a vehement passion of divine love is the fruit of these sharp afflictions of the soul

1. Foretaste of God in the night of the spirit.
2. Love of God infused into the purified soul.
3. Continuation.
4. Continuation.
5. Concentration of powers of the soul on God.
6. No satiety in divine love.
7. Anxious longing of the soul for God.
8. Its causes: spiritual darkness and infused love of God.

With anxious love inflamed,

In this line the soul speaks of the fire of love of which we have spoken, and which, in the night of painful contemplation, seizes upon it as material fire on the fuel it burns. This burning, though in a certain way resembling that which, as we explained before, takes place in the sensual part of the soul, is still, in one sense, as different from this, of which I am now speaking, as the soul is from the body, the spiritual from the sensual. For this is a certain fire of love in the spirit whereby the soul, amidst these dark trials, feels itself wounded to the quick by this strong love divine with a certain sense and foretaste of God, though it understands nothing distinctly, because, as I have said, the understanding is in darkness.

2. The spirit is now conscious of deep love, for this spiritual

burning produces the passion of it. And inasmuch as this love is infused passively rather than actively, the soul corresponds only passively with it, and thus a strong passion of love is begotten within it. This love has in it something of the most perfect union with God, and thus partakes in some measure of its properties, which are more especially actions of God received in the soul rather than of the soul, in which they subsist passively, the soul giving its consent thereto.

3. But this warmth and force and temper and passion of love, or burning, as the soul calls it, are solely the work of God Who is entering into union with it. The more the desires are restrained, subdued, and disabled for the enjoyment of the things of heaven and earth, the more room does this love find in the soul, and better the dispositions for its reception, so that it may unite itself with that soul, and wound it. This takes place, as has been said before, during the dark purgation in a wonderful way, for God has so weaned the faculties, and they are now so recollected in Him, that they are unable to take pleasure as they like in anything whatever.

4. All this is the work of God, wrought with a view to withdraw the faculties of the soul from all objects whatever, and to concentrate them upon Himself, that the soul may acquire greater strength and fitness for the strong union of love of God which He is communicating in the purgative way; and in which the soul must love Him with all its strength and desire of sense and spirit, which it could never do if the faculties thereof were dissipated by other satisfactions. The Psalmist, therefore, that he might be able to receive this strong love of the union with God, said unto Him, 'I will keep my strength for Thee;' that is, all my capacity and desires, the strength of my faculties, neither will I suffer them to do or rejoice in anything but Thee.

5. Here we may perceive, in some degree, how great and how vehement is this burning of love in the spirit when God gathers and collects together all the strength, faculties, and desires of the soul, both spiritual and sensual, so that all this unison may use all its energies and all its forces in this love, and so come to satisfy truly, and in perfection, the first commandment, which, neglecting nothing that

belongs to man, and shutting out nothing that is his from this love, saith, namely, 'Thou shalt love the Lord thy God with thy whole heart, and with thy whole soul, and with thy whole strength.'

6. When all the desires and energies of the soul are thus recollected in this burning of love, and the soul itself touched, wounded, and set on fire with love, in them all, what must the movements and affections of these desires and energies be when they are thus wounded and burning in this strong love, when that love does not satiate them, when they are in darkness and doubt about it, and suffering also, beyond all question, a more grievous hunger, like the dogs which, as David says, not finding their fill of this love, 'go round about the city howling and crying'. For the touch of this love and of the divine fire so dries up the spirit, and enkindles its longing to satisfy its thirst, that it turns upon itself a thousand times, and longs for God in a thousand ways, as David did when he said, 'For Thee my soul hath thirsted, for Thee my flesh, O how many ways'; that is, in desire. Another version reads, 'My soul thirsteth after Thee, my soul is dying for Thee.'

7. This is the reason why the soul says, 'With anxious love inflamed.' In all its works and thoughts, in all its employments and on every occasion, the soul loves and longs in many ways, and this longing also is manifold in its forms, always and everywhere present; the soul has no rest, feeling itself to be wounded and on fire with anxious love; its state is thus described by holy Job: 'As a servant desireth the shadow, as the hired man tarrieth for the end of his work, so I also have had vain months, and have numbered to myself laborious nights. If I sleep, I shall say, When shall I arise? and again I shall expect the evening, and shall be replenished with sorrows even until darkness.' The soul is discontented with itself, with heaven and with earth, being replenished with sorrows even until the darkness of which Job is here speaking. That darkness, speaking in a spiritual sense, and according to the matter which I am discussing, is distress and suffering without the comfort of any certain hope of any light and spiritual good.

8. The anxieties and sufferings of the soul while thus on fire with

love are the greater, because of their two-fold origin; the spiritual darkness which envelops it is one, and that afflicts it with doubts and misgivings. The love of God which sets it on fire is the other, which stirs it with the wound of love and makes it burn marvellously. These two kinds of suffering are thus referred to by Isaias, being in a like condition: 'My soul hath desired Thee in the night'; that is, in misery. This is one kind of pain which proceeds from the dark night, 'Yea, and with my spirit in my heart I will watch to Thee in the morning.' This is the other kind of suffering in desire and anxiety, which proceeds from love, in the bowels of the spirit; that is, the spiritual affections. The soul, however, amidst these gloomy and loving pains, is conscious of a certain companionship and inward strength which attends upon it and so invigorates it that if the burden of this oppressive darkness be removed, it oftentimes feels itself desolate, empty, and weak. The reason is that the force and courage communicated to the soul flow passively from the dark fire of love which assails it, and so, when that fire ceases to assail it, the darkness, the strength, and fire of love at the same time cease in the soul.

CHAPTER XII

Shows how this awful night is a purgatory, and how in it the divine wisdom illuminates men on earth with that light in which the angels are purified and enlightened in heaven

1. Two purgatories.
2. The infused wisdom of love.
3. Infused love and knowledge of the angels.
4. Of men.
5. Increasing in holiness is advancing in knowledge.
6. Joy of the union of intellect and will in God.

What I have said will enable us to see how the dark night of loving fire purifies in the darkness, and how the soul in the darkness is set on fire. We shall also see that, as the dark and material fires in the next life purify the spirit, so the loving, dark, and spiritual fires here, purify and cleanse the soul. The difference is that in the next world they are purified by fire, and here, purified and enlightened by love. David prayed for this love when he said, 'Create a clean heart in me, O God!' for cleanness of heart is nothing else but the love and grace of God. 'The clean of heart,' are called blessed by our Saviour, and it is as if He had said, blessed are those who love, for blessedness can come of nothing less than love.

2. The following words of Jeremias, 'From on high He hath cast a fire in my bones, and hath taught me,' show plainly that the soul is purified when it is enlightened in the fire of loving wisdom, for God never grants the mystical wisdom without love; it being love itself

that infuses it into the soul. David also saith that the wisdom of God is silver tried in the purifying fire of love; 'words of our Lord are chaste words, silver examined by fire,' for the dim contemplation infuses into the soul love and wisdom, in every one according to its necessity and capacity, enlightening the soul, and cleansing it of all its ignorances, according to the words of the Wise Man, 'He hath enlightened my ignorances.'

3. Here, also, we learn that the wisdom which purifies the ignorances of the angels (giving them knowledge, enlightening them on what they are ignorant of), flowing from God through the highest, down to the lowest, in the order of the heavenly hierarchy, and thence to men, is that very wisdom which purifies these souls and enlightens them. All the works of the angels, and all the inspirations they suggest, are, therefore, in Holy Scripture, truly and properly said to be their work and God's work: for, ordinarily, His inspirations come through the angels; they receiving them one from another simultaneously, as the light of the sun penetrates many windows at once, arranged one behind the other. For though it is true that the light of the sun pierces all, yet each window conveys and pours that light into the next, somewhat modified, according to the nature of the glass; somewhat weaker and fainter, according to the distance from the sun.

4. Hence it follows, with respect to the higher and lower angels, the nearer they are to God the more they are purified and enlightened in the general purgation; the lowest in rank receiving their illumination in a less perfect degree. But man, being the last in order to whom this loving contemplation is to be granted, must receive that enlightenment according to his capacity in a limited degree, and with suffering. For the light of God which illumines an angel enlightens him, and sets him on fire with love, for he is a spirit already prepared for the infusion of that light; but man, being impure and weak, is ordinarily enlightened, as I said before, in darkness, in distress and pain – the sun's rays are painful in their light to weak eyes – till the fire of love, purifying him, shall have spiritualized and refined him, so that being made pure he may be able to

receive with sweetness, like the angels, the union of this inflowing love, as we shall explain, with the help of our Lord; but, in the meantime, this contemplation and loving knowledge come upon the soul through trials and loving anxiety, of which I am now speaking.

5. The soul is not always conscious of this burning and anxious love; for in the beginning of the spiritual purgation all the divine fire is employed in drying up and preparing the soul, rather than in setting it on fire. But when, in course of time, the soul has become heated in the fire, it then feels most commonly this burning and warmth of love. And now, as the understanding is being purified more and more in this darkness, it happens occasionally that this mystical and affective theology, while inflaming the will, wounds also by enlightening the other faculty of the understanding with a certain divine light and knowledge, so sweetly and so divinely, that the will, aided by it though inactive, glows in a marvellous manner, the divine fire of love burning within it with living flames, so that the soul appears to have received a living fire with a living understanding. This is what David referred to when he said, 'My heart waxed hot within me, and in my meditation a fire shall burn, so vehemently that I thought it to be already on fire.'

6. This kindling of love, in the union of these two powers, the understanding and the will, is to the soul a great treasure and delight, because it is a certain touch of the Godhead and the foundation of the perfection of the union of love, for which the soul hopes. Thus the soul does not reach this sublime sense and love of God without passing through many tribulations, and accomplishing a great part of its purgation. But for other degrees of this union, lower than this, which are of ordinary occurrence, so intense a purgation is not required. From what we have said here it follows that these spiritual treasures, being passively infused into the soul by God, the will indeed may love and yet the understanding not understand, and likewise the understanding may be active while the will remains without love; for as the dark night of contemplation comprises both divine light and love, just as fire which has light and heat, it is not surprising that this loving light sometimes striking the will

enkindles in it love, the understanding meanwhile remaining in darkness because the light has not fallen on it; at other times the light striking the understanding enlightens it and bestows knowledge on it while leaving the will dry, just as one might perceive the heat of fire without seeing its light, or the light without feeling any warmth, for it is the Lord who acts thus, infusing His gifts as He likes.

CHAPTER XIII

Other sweet effects wrought in the soul in the dark night
of contemplation

1. Illumination of the intellect. Pure spiritual affections
    of the will.
2. Thirst of love.
3. Appreciative love of God.
4. Strength of it.
5. St Mary Magdalene. Love inebriates.
6. Love thinks all things possible.
7. Love impatient.
8. Conscious unworthiness reconciled with ardent aspi-
    ration.
9. Misery of the soul seen in the divine light.
10. Growth of sight.
11. Great mercy of God in restoring youth to the soul.
12. Intellect, will, and memory born anew.
13. and 14. Conclusion.

By the expression 'burning' we understand some of the sweet effects
which are wrought in the soul by the dark night of contemplation;
for occasionally, amid the darkness, the soul receives light – 'light
shineth in darkness' – the mystical inflowing streaming directly into
the understanding, while the will remains dry, that is, not reaching
to actual union, but with a calmness and pureness so exquisite and so
delicious to the soul as to be utterly indescribable: now God is felt to
be present in one way, and again in another. Sometimes, too, it

wounds the will at the same time, and enkindles love deeply, tenderly, and strongly; for, as I have said that sometimes these two faculties unite themselves, the more the understanding is purified the more perfect and delicate, at times, is the union of the understanding and the will. But, before the soul attains to this state, it is more common for the touch of the fire of love to be felt in the will than for the touch of the perfect intelligence to be felt in the understanding.

Why, then, one might ask, if these two faculties are purified together, does one at the beginning generally feel the will to be inflamed with the love of purifying contemplation, rather than the mind with the understanding of it? The answer is, that here this passive love does not directly strike the will but the substance of the soul, thus moving the affections passively; for the will is a free faculty, whereas this burning love is a passion rather than a free act of the will. It is therefore called passion of love, and not a free act, because such an act is only in so far an act of the will as it is free. But as these passions and affections belong to the will it is correct to say that the will is subject to a passionate affection when the soul is subject to it, for in this manner the will is made captive, losing its liberty, being carried away by the impetuous force of the passion. In this sense one may say that this burning love is in the will, that is, it inflames the appetite of the will, and thus, as already stated, it is more properly called a passion of love than a free act of the will. On the other hand, the receptive passion of the understanding can only receive knowledge purely and passively – and this only when it has been purified – therefore previous to purgation the soul feels less frequently the touch of knowledge than the passion of love, for this latter does not require that the soul should be so thoroughly purified concerning its passions, since these precisely help it in feeling passionate love.

2. This burning, and thirst of love, inasmuch as it now proceeds from the Holy Ghost, is very different from that of which I spoke in describing the night of sense. For though sense also has now its part in this, because it cannot but share in the afflictions of the spirit, yet

the root and living force of the thirst of love are felt in the higher part of the soul, that is, in the spirit. The spirit perceives and understands what it feels, and that it possesses not that which it longs for, so that it counts as nothing all the pain it feels, though it is beyond comparison greater than the pain of the first night, which is the night of sense; for it thoroughly understands that one great good is absent, and that there is no remedy possible.

3. It may be observed here that, although at first, in the beginning of the spiritual night, this burning love is not felt because the fire of love has not yet done its work, God communicates to the soul, instead of it, a reverent love of Himself so great that, as I have said, the heaviest trials and deepest afflictions of this night are the distressing thought that it has lost God, and that He has abandoned it. It may, therefore, be always said that from the beginning of this night the soul is full of the anxieties of love, at one time that of reverence, at another that of burning. It is evident that the greatest of its sufferings is this doubt: for if it could be persuaded that all is not lost and over, and that the trials it undergoes are, as in truth they are, for its greater good, and that God is not angry, it would make no account whatever of all these afflictions; on the contrary, it would rejoice, knowing that by them it is serving God.

4. This reverential love of God is so strong in the soul – though in the darkness and unaware of it – that it would be glad not only to endure its trials but also to die a thousand deaths to serve Him. But when the fire of love and the reverent love of God together have set the soul in a flame, it is wont to gain such strength and energy, and such eager longing after God – effects of this glowing love – that it boldly disregards all considerations, and sets everything aside, in the inebriating force of love, and, without much consideration of its acts, it conducts itself strangely and extravagantly in every way that it may come to Him whom the soul loveth.

5. This is the reason why Mary Magdalene, though so noble, heeded not the many guests, high and low, who were feasting, as we read in St Luke, in the house of the Pharisee. She considered not that she was not welcome, and that tears were unseemly at the feast,

provided she could, without an hour's delay, or waiting for another occasion, reach Him for whom her soul was wounded and on fire. This is that inebriating and daring force of love, which, when she knew that her Love was in the sepulchre, guarded by soldiers lest the disciples should take Him away, and a stone rolled over it and sealed, allowed none of these things to move her; for she went thither before dawn with the ointments to anoint her Beloved. And, finally, it was under the inebriating influence and anxieties of love that she asked Himself, Whom she took for the gardener, who, she thought, had robbed the sepulchre, to tell her, if he had taken Him away, where he had laid Him. 'If thou hast carried Him away, tell me where thou hast laid Him, and I will take Him away.' She did not reflect upon the imprudence of her words; for it is clear that if the gardener had stolen the Body he would not have told her, still less would he have allowed her to take Him away.

6. This conduct of Mary Magdalene proceeded from the vehemence and energy of her love; for love thinks all things possible, and that all are of the same mind with itself; for it cannot believe that there is anything to occupy men, or anything to be sought for by them, except that which itself seeks and loves; it considers that there can be no other occupation or desire except its own, and that every one should busy himself in this. Thus, when the bride went out into the streets and highways seeking her beloved, she, believing that all were employed, like herself, in searching for him, adjured them, if they found him, to tell him that she languished with love.

7. So strong was Mary's love that she intended, if the gardener had told her where he had hidden our Lord, to go and take Him away, in spite of any prohibition. Of this kind are those anxieties of love which the soul feels when it has made some progress in the spiritual purgation. The soul rises by night – that is, in the purifying darkness – in the affections of the will. As a lioness or a bear, robbed of its whelps, whom it cannot find, seeks them anxiously and earnestly, so does the wounded soul seek after God. Being in darkness, it feels His absence, and is dying of love. This is that impatient love which no man can endure long without obtaining his wishes or

dying. It is like Rachel's longing for children, when she said to Jacob, 'Give me children, otherwise I shall die.'

8. We have now to consider how it is that the soul, conscious of its own misery and unworthiness before God, can be so bold, amid the purifying darkness, as to aspire after union with Him. The reason is, that love gives it strength to love in earnest, it being the nature of love to seek for union, companionship, equality with, and likeness to the object beloved, so as to attain to the perfection of itself. Hence it is that the soul not yet made perfect in love, because it has not attained to union, hungers and thirsts for that which it has not – namely, union; and the strength which love communicates to the will, which is on fire, renders it bold and daring as to the will, though as to the understanding, because that is in darkness, it feels itself to be an unworthy and miserable object.

9. I must not omit here to say why it is that the divine light, being always light to the soul, does not illumine it the moment it strikes it, as it does at a later time, instead of bringing with it the darkness and misery of which I am speaking. Something has been already said, but I now speak of it directly. The darkness and other miseries of which the soul is conscious proceed not from the divine light when it strikes the soul, but from the soul itself, and it is the light which enables it to see them. The divine light gives light at once, but the soul sees nothing at first but that which is immediately before it, or rather within itself; its own darkness and misery, which, by the mercy of God, it sees now, and formerly saw not, because this super-natural light had not been granted it.

10. This is the reason why, in the beginning, the soul is conscious of nothing but of darkness and misery. But when it has been purified by the knowledge and sense of its misery it will have eyes to discern the blessings of the divine light, and being delivered and set free from all darkness and imperfections, the great blessings and profit will become known which the soul is gaining for itself in this blessed night.

11. This shows how great is the mercy of God to the soul when He thus purifies it in this strong lye and bitter purgation, as to its

sensual and spiritual part, from all its affections and imperfect habits in all that relates to time, nature, sense, and spirit; by darkening its interior faculties, and emptying them of all objects, by correcting and drying up all affections of sense and spirit, by weakening and wasting the natural forces, which the soul never could have done of itself, as we shall immediately show. God makes it die, in this way, to all that is not God, that, being denuded and stripped of its former clothing, it may clothe itself anew. Thus the soul's 'youth shall be renewed like the eagle's', clothed with 'the new man, which, in the words of the Apostle, is created according to God in justice.'

12. Now this is nothing else but the supernatural light giving light to the understanding, so that the human understanding becomes divine, made one with the divine. In the same way divine love inflames the will so that it becomes nothing less than divine, loving in a divine way, united and made one with the divine will and divine love. The memory is affected in like manner; all the desires and affections also are changed divinely according to God. Thus the soul will be of heaven, heavenly, divine rather than human.

13. All this, as is clear from what I have said, is the work of God in the soul during this night, enlightening it and setting it on fire in a divine way with an anxious solicitude for God alone, and for naught besides.

14. It is with great propriety and justice, therefore, that the soul repeats the third line of the stanza, which, together with those that follow, I repeat again and explain in the following chapter.

CHAPTER XIV

Repeats and explains the last three lines of the first stanza

1. The soul leaves the house of self-indulgence.
2. The passions subdued, the soul goes forth to God.
3. Happiness of such a soul.

> *O happy lot!*
> *Forth unobserved I went,*
> *My house being now at rest.*

The happy lot of which the soul is singing in the first of these three lines befell it through those means of which it speaks in the two lines that follow it; making use of a metaphor, it describes itself as one who, for the better execution of his purpose, goes out of his house by night, in the dark, the inmates of which are at rest, in order that none might hinder him. The soul having to perform so heroic and so rare an act, that of being united to the divine Beloved, sallies forth, because the Beloved is to be found only without, in solitude. The bride therefore desired to find Him alone, saying: 'Who shall give Thee to me for my brother, sucking the breasts of my mother, that I may find Thee without and kiss Thee?' It is necessary for the enamoured soul, in order to obtain the end desired, to act in the same way; to go out by night when all the inmates of its house repose and sleep; that is, when its lower operations, passions, and desires are at rest and asleep in this night. These are the inmates of its house which when awake ever hinder its good, enemies of its freedom. These are they of whom our Saviour said in the holy Gospel, 'A man's enemies shall be they of his own household!'

2. Thus it is necessary that their operations and motions should be lulled to sleep in this night in order that they may be no hindrance to the supernatural blessings of union with God in love, for while they continue to energize and act, that is unattainable. All movement and action on their part, instead of helping, hinder the reception of the spiritual blessings of the union of love, because all natural exertion is defective with regard to those supernatural blessings which God alone secretly and silently infuses into the passive soul. Hence it is necessary that the powers of the soul should be at rest, keeping passive, if it is to receive what God infuses, and should not interfere with their own inferior actions and base inclinations.

3. It was a happy lot for the soul when God in this night put all its household to sleep, that is, all the powers, passions, affections, and desires of the sensual and spiritual soul, that it may attain to the spiritual union of the perfect love of God 'unobserved', that is, unhindered by these affections – now lulled and mortified in the dark of this night that they may notice or feel naught according to their mean nature whereby to prevent the soul from going forth from self and the habitation of sensuality. O how happy must the soul then be, when it can escape from the house of its sensuality! None can understand it, I think, except that soul which has experienced it. That soul clearly sees how wretched was its former slavery, and how great its misery when it lay at the mercy of its passions and desires; it learns now that the life of the spirit is true liberty and riches, with innumerable blessings in its train, some of which I shall speak of while explaining the following stanzas, when it will more clearly appear what good reasons the soul has for describing the passage of this awful night as a happy lot.

Chapter XV

The second stanza and its explanation

Answer to an objection.

> *In darkness and in safety,*
> *By the secret ladder, disguised,*
> *O happy lot!*
> *In darkness and concealment,*
> *My house being now at rest.*

In this stanza the soul goes on singing still of certain properties of the darkness of this night, speaking again of the happy lot which befell it through them. It speaks of them in answering an implied objection, observing that no one is to think that because in this dark night it passed through so many storms of affliction, doubt, fear, and horror, as I said before, it had therefore run any risk of being lost; yea, rather, it found safety in the darkness, because in the darkness it was free and skilfully escaped from its enemies who were ever hindering its departure.

2. In the darkness of the night it changed its garments, and disguised itself in three colours, of which I shall speak hereafter. It sallied forth unknown to the whole of its household by a most secret ladder, which, as I shall show in the proper place, is a living faith – in such secrecy and silence, for the better execution of its purpose, that it could not possibly be in greater security; especially now, because in the purgative night the desires, passions, and affections of the soul are asleep, mortified, and subdued; and these are they which, awake and active, would never have consented to that departure.

Chapter XVI

Showeth how the soul journeys securely when in darkness

1. Means of the safe journey in the spiritual night.
2. Security found in self-mortification.
3. Man destroys, God saves.
4. Gains.
5. Why are the natural faculties obscured?
6. Because in themselves incapable of perfect union with God.
7. Natural taste and facility not spiritual fervour.
8. The soul delivered from itself and prepared for God.
9. Four reasons why the dark road is safe: God is the guide.
10. Suffering gives strength.
11. The way enlightened by divine wisdom.
12. The soul guarded by the obscurity of divine contemplation.
13. Texts.
14. One of the miseries of this life is the difficulty in knowing truth.
15. God the tabernacle of protection.
16. Fourth reason: courage and vigilance acquired at the outset.

In darkness and in safety,

The darkness of which the soul here speaks relates, as I have said, to the desires and powers of sense, interior and spiritual, all of which are deprived of their natural light in this night, that, being purified as to this, they may be supernaturally enlightened. The desires of sense and spirit are lulled to sleep and mortified, unable to relish anything either human or divine; the affections of the soul are thwarted and brought low, become helpless, and have nothing to rest upon; the imagination is fettered, and unable to make any profitable reflections, the memory is gone, and the will, too, is dry and afflicted, and all the faculties are empty and useless, and, moreover, a dense and heavy cloud overshadows the soul, distresses it and holds it as if it were far away from God. This is the darkness in which the soul says that it travels in safety.

2. The reason of this safety has been clearly shown: for usually the soul never errs, except under the influence of its desires, or tastes, or reflections, or understanding, or affections, wherein it generally is over-abundant, or defective, changeable, or inconsistent; hence the inclination to that which is not becoming. It is therefore clear that the soul is secure against being led astray by them, when all these operations and movements have ceased. Because then the soul is delivered, not only from itself, but also from its other enemies – the world and the devil – who, when the affections and operations of the soul have ceased, cannot assault it by any other way or by any other means.

3. It follows from this, that the greater the darkness and emptiness of its natural operations in which the soul travels, the greater is its security. For as the prophet saith, 'Perdition is thine own, O Israel; only in Me is thy help.' The perdition of the soul is exclusively its own work – the result of its own operations, of its unsubdued desires, interior and sensual – and its salvation, saith God, cometh from Me only. When the soul is hindered from giving way to its imperfections there descend upon it forthwith the blessings of union with God, in its desires and faculties which that union will render heavenly and divine.

4. If, therefore, while this darkness lasts, the soul will look within, it will very clearly see how slightly the desires and the faculties have

been diverted towards vain and unprofitable matters, and that it is secure itself against vainglory, pride, and presumption, empty rejoicing, and many other evils. It is quite clear, therefore, that the soul which is in this darkness is not only not lost, but that it gains much, for now it acquires virtue.

5. But here a question arises: Why is it – seeing that the things of God are profitable and beneficial to the soul, and a source of security – that the desires and faculties are so darkened by Him in this night that they cannot have any joy in spiritual things or occupy themselves with them as with other things, but are, in some way, less able to do so? To this I reply, that it is then profitable for the soul not to act and be devoid of pleasure even in spiritual things, seeing that its faculties and desires are base and impure and altogether natural; and even if they have pleasure in, and are familiar with, divine and supernatural things, that can be so only in their naturally mean way.

6. It is a philosophical axiom that all that is received is received according to the condition of the recipient. From this it follows that the natural faculties – being without the requisite purity, strength, and capacity for the reception and fruition of divine things in their way, which is divine, but only in their own, which is human and vile – must be in darkness with regard to the divine way, so as to secure their perfect purgation. That being weaned, purified, and brought to nothing, they may lose their own mode of acting and receiving, and may be thus disposed and tempered for the reception and fruition of that which is divine in a high and noble way; which cannot be if the old man do not die first. Hence it is that all spiritual graces if they do not descend from the Father of lights upon the human will and desire, however much a man may exercise his taste, desire, and faculties about God, and however much he may seem to succeed, are still not divinely nor spiritually enjoyed, but humanly and naturally like all other things, for these are not goods flowing from man to God, but coming to man from God.

7. As to this I might here show, were this the proper place, that there are many whose tastes and affections, and the operations of whose faculties, are directed to God and to spiritual things, who may

imagine all this to be supernatural and spiritual, when in reality it is nothing more, perhaps, than acts and desires most natural and human. As they regard ordinary matters, so also do they regard good things, with a certain natural facility which they have in directing their faculties and desires to anything, whatever it may be. If I can find an opportunity in the course of this discussion, I propose to enter upon this question, and describe some of the signs by which we may know when the motives and interior acts of the soul in the things of God are natural only, when they are spiritual only, and when they are natural and spiritual together. It is enough for us here to know that the interior acts and movements of the soul, if they are to be divinely influenced by God, must be first of all lulled to sleep, darkened and subdued, in their natural state, so far as their capacity and operations are concerned, until they lose all their strength.

8. O spiritual soul, when thou seest thy desire obscured, thy will arid and constrained, and thy faculties incapable of any interior act, be not grieved at this, but look upon it rather as a great good, for God is delivering thee from thyself, taking the matter out of thy hands; for however strenuously thou mayest exert thyself, thou wilt never do anything so faultlessly, perfectly, and securely as now – because of the impurity and torpor of thy faculties – when God, taking thee by the hand, is guiding thee in the dark as one that is blind, along a road and to an end thou knowest not, and whither thou couldst never travel by the help of thine own eyes and thine own feet, however strong thou mayest be.

9. The reason why the soul not only travels securely when it thus travels in the dark, but makes even greater progress, is this: In general the soul makes greater progress when it least thinks so, yea, most frequently when it imagines that it is losing. Having never before experienced the present novelty which dazzles it, and disturbs its former habits, it considers itself as losing, rather than as gaining ground, when it sees itself lost in a place it once knew, and in which it delighted, travelling by a road it knows not, and in which it has no pleasure. As a traveller into strange countries goes by ways strange and untried, relying on information derived from others,

and not upon any knowledge of his own – it is clear that he will never reach a new country but by new ways which he knows not, and by abandoning those he knew – so in the same way the soul makes the greater progress when it travels in the dark, not knowing the way. But inasmuch as God Himself is here the guide of the soul in its blindness, the soul may well exult and say, 'In darkness and in safety,' now that it has come to a knowledge of its state.

10. There is another reason also why the soul has travelled safely in this obscurity; it has suffered: for the way of suffering is safer, and also more profitable, than that of rejoicing and of action. In suffering God gives strength, but in action and in joy the soul does but show its own weakness and imperfections. And in suffering, the soul practises and acquires virtue, and becomes purer, wiser, and more cautious.

11. There is another and stronger reason why the soul travels securely when in darkness. This reason is derived from the consideration of the light itself, or dark wisdom. The dark night of contemplation so absorbs the soul, and brings it so near unto God, that He defends it, and delivers it from all that is not God. For the soul is now, as it were, under medical treatment for the recovery of its health, which is God Himself: God compels it to observe a particular diet, and to abstain from all hurtful things, the very desire for them being subdued. The soul is treated like a sick man respected by his household, who is so carefully tended that the air shall not touch him, nor the light shine upon him, whom the noise of footsteps and the tumult of servants shall not disturb, and to whom the most delicate food is given most cautiously by measure, and that nutritious rather than savoury.

12. All these advantages – they all minister to the safe-keeping of the soul – are the effects of this dim contemplation, for it brings the soul nearer to God. The truth is, that the nearer the soul comes to Him it perceives that darkness is greater and deeper because of its own weakness; thus the nearer the sun the greater the darkness and distress wrought by its great brightness, because our eyes are weak, imperfect, and defective. Hence it is that the spiritual light of God is

so immeasurable, so far above the understanding, that when it comes near to it, it dims and blinds it.

13. This is the reason why David said that God made darkness His hiding-place and covert, His tabernacle around Him, dark water in the clouds of the air. The dark water in the clouds of the air is the dim contemplation and divine wisdom in souls, as I am going to explain, of which they have experience as a thing near to the pavilion where He dwells, when God brings them nearer to Himself. Thus, that which in God is light and supreme splendour, is to man thick darkness, as St Paul saith, and as the royal prophet David explains it in the same psalm, saying: 'Because of the brightness of His presence the clouds passed,' that is, clouds and darkness over the natural understanding, 'the light of which', saith the prophet Isaias, 'is darkened in the mist thereof.'

14. O wretched condition of this life wherein it is so dangerous to live and so difficult to find the truth! That which is most clear and true, is to us most obscure and doubtful, and we therefore avoid it though it is most necessary for us. That which shines the most, and dazzles our eyes, that we embrace and follow after, though it is most hurtful to us, and makes us stumble at every step. In what fear and danger then must man be living, seeing that the very light of his natural eyes, by which he directs his steps, is the very first to bewilder and deceive him when he would draw near unto God. If he wishes to be sure of the road he travels on, he must close his eyes and walk in the dark, if he is to journey in safety from his domestic foes, which are his own senses and faculties.

15. Well hidden and protected then is the soul in the dark waters close to God. For as the dark waters are a tabernacle and dwelling-place for God Himself, so they are also to the soul perfect safety and protection, though in darkness, where it is hidden and protected from itself, as I have said, and from all the injuries that created things may afflict. It is of souls thus protected that David spoke when he said in another psalm: 'Thou shalt hide them in the secret of Thy face, from the disturbance of men. Thou shalt protect them in Thy tabernacle from the contradiction of tongues.' These words

comprehend all kinds of protection; for to be hidden 'in the secret of the face' of God 'from the disturbance of men', is to be strengthened in the dim contemplation against all the assaults of men. To be protected in His 'tabernacle from the contradiction of tongues', is to be engulfed in the dark waters, which is the tabernacle of which David speaks. That soul, therefore, whose desires and affections are weaned, and whose faculties are in darkness, is set free from all the imperfections which war against the spirit, whether they proceed from the flesh, or from any other created thing. The soul, therefore, may well say, 'In darkness and in safety'.

16. Another reason, not less conclusive, why the soul, though in darkness, travels securely, is derived from that courage which it acquires as soon as it enters within the dark, painful, and gloomy waters of God. Though it be dark, still it is water, and therefore cannot but refresh and strengthen the soul in all that is most necessary for it, though it does so painfully and in darkness. For the soul immediately discerns in itself a certain courage and resolution to do nothing which it knows to be displeasing unto God, and to leave nothing undone which ministers to His service, because this love, which is dim, is most watchful and careful of what it is to do, and what it is to leave undone, for His sake, so as to please Him. It looks around and considers in a thousand ways whether it has done anything to offend Him, and all this with much more solicitude and carefulness than it ever did before, as I said when speaking of this anxious love. Here all the desires, all the strength, and all the powers of the soul, recollected from all besides, direct all their efforts and all their energies to the service of God only. Thus the soul goes forth out of itself, away from all created things, to the sweet and delightsome union of the love of God, 'in darkness and in safety'.

CHAPTER XVII

Gives the second line and explains how this dim contemplation is secret

1. Three points of explanation: secret, ladder, disguised.
2. Secret.
3. Continuation.
4. Nature of divine language.
5. Jeremias and Moses.
6. Difficulties of contemplation with their directors.
7. The soul hidden in the abyss of wisdom.
8. Continuation.
9. It leads the soul to union with a hidden God.
10. Contemplation an infusion of the secret wisdom of God.

By the secret ladder, disguised,

I have three things to explain in reference to the three words of this line. Two of them – 'secret' and 'ladder' – belong to the dark night of contemplation of which I am speaking, but the third – 'disguised' – belongs to the way of the soul therein. As to the first, the soul calls the dim contemplation, by which it goes forth to the union of love, a secret ladder, and that because of two properties of it which I am going to explain, namely, that it is secret, and that it is a ladder. First, this dark contemplation is called secret, because it is, as I have said before, the mystical theology which theologians call secret wisdom, and which, according to St Thomas, is infused into the soul more especially by love. This happens in a secret hidden way in which the natural operations of the understanding and the other faculties have no share. And, therefore, because the faculties of the soul cannot compass it, it being the Holy Ghost Who infuses it into the soul, in a way it knoweth not, as the bride saith in the Canticle, we call it secret.

2. And, in truth, it is not the soul only that knows it not, but every one else, even the devil; because the Master who now teaches the soul dwells substantially within it, whither Satan cannot penetrate, neither the natural senses nor the understanding. This is not the only reason why it is called secret, for it is secret also in its effects. It is not only secret beyond the powers of the soul to speak of it, during the darkness and sharpness of the purgation, when the secret wisdom is purifying the soul, but afterwards also, during the illumination, when that wisdom is most clearly communicated, it is so secret that it cannot be discerned or described. Moreover, the soul has no wish to speak of it, and besides, it can discover no way or proper similitude to describe it by, so as to make known a knowledge so high, a spiritual impression so delicate and infused. Yea, and if it could have a wish to speak of it, and find terms to describe it, it would always remain secret still.

3. Because this interior wisdom is so simple, general, and spiritual, that it enters not into the understanding under any form or image subject to sense, as is sometimes the case, the imagination, therefore, and the senses — as it has not entered in by them, nor is modified by them — cannot account for it, nor form any conception of it, so as to speak in any degree correctly about it, though the soul be distinctly conscious that it feels and tastes this sweet and strange wisdom. The soul is like a man who sees an object for the first time, the like of which he has never seen before; he handles it and feels it, yet he cannot say what it is, or tell its name, do what he may, though it be at the same time an object cognizable by the senses. How much less then can that be described which does not enter in by the senses?

4. Such is the nature of the divine language that the more interior, infused, and spiritual it is, the more it transcends every sense; the

powers of the senses, interior and exterior, cease, and their harmonies become mute.

5. The Holy Writings supply both proofs and illustrations of this principle. Jeremias shows the impossibility of manifesting and expressing it in words: for when God had spoken to him he knew not what to say, except, 'Ah, ah, ah, Lord God.' Moses, also, is an instance of the interior helplessness, that is, of the interior imaginative sense, and of the exterior also at the same time: for when God spoke to him out of the bush, he not only saw that he could not speak, but, as is said in the Acts of the Apostles, he 'durst not behold', that is, with the interior imagination, which he considered far removed and powerless not only to form some picture of what he saw in God, but not even capable of receiving an impression thereof. Hence, inasmuch as the wisdom of this contemplation is the language of God addressed to the soul, as of a pure Spirit speaking to another pure spirit, nothing inferior to a spirit, such as the senses, is able to perceive it; it remains, therefore, a secret to them which they neither know nor can express, nor do they wish to know it because they do not even see it.

6. This explains why some persons, walking in this way, good and timid souls, who, when they would give an account of their interior state to their directors, know not how to do it, neither have they the power to do it, and so feel a great repugnance to explain themselves, especially when contemplation is the more simple and with difficulty discernible by them. All they can say is that their soul is satisfied, calm, or contented, that they have a sense of the presence of God, and that all goes well with them, as they think; but they cannot explain their state, except by general expressions of this kind. But it is a different matter when they have a consciousness of particular things, such as visions, impressions, and the like; these in general are communicated under some species, in which the senses participate; in that case they are able to describe them. But it is not in the nature of pure contemplation that it can be described; for it can scarcely be spoken of in words, and therefore we call it secret.

7. This is not the only reason why it is called secret, and why it is

so. There is another, namely the mystical wisdom has the property of hiding the soul within itself. For besides its ordinary operation, it sometimes so absorbs the soul and plunges it in this secret abyss that the soul sees itself distinctly as far away from, and abandoned by, all created things; it looks upon itself as one that is placed in a wild and vast solitude whither no human being can come, as in an immense wilderness without limits; a wilderness, the more delicious, sweet, and lovely, the more it is wide, vast, and lonely, where the soul is the more hidden, the more it is raised up above all created things.

8. This abyss of wisdom now so exalts and elevates the soul – orderly disposing it for the science of love – that it makes it not only understand how mean are all created things in relation to the supreme wisdom and divine knowledge, but also, how low, defective, and, in a certain sense, improper, are all the words and phrases by which in this life we discuss divine things, and how utterly impossible by any natural means, however profoundly and learnedly we may speak, to understand and see them as they are, except in the light of mystical theology. And so the soul in the light thereof discerning this truth, namely, that it cannot reach it, and still less explain it by the terms of ordinary speech, justly calls it secret.

9. This property of being secret, and of surpassing all natural capacity, belongs to divine contemplation, not only because it is itself supernatural, but also because it is the guide of the soul to the perfections of union with God, which not being humanly known, we must reach by not knowing the way humanly, and being divinely ignorant. For, to use the language of mystical theology, as we are doing, these divine perfections are neither understood nor known when they are sought, but when they are found and practised. For thus the prophet Baruch speaks of the divine wisdom: 'There is none that can know her ways, nor that can search out her paths.' The royal prophet also, speaking of this way of the soul, says unto God: 'Thy lightnings enlightened the round world, the earth was moved and trembled, Thy way is in the sea, and Thy paths in many waters, and Thy steps shall not be known.' All this in a spiritual sense explains the matter I am discussing.

10. The lightnings that enlightened the round world is the illumination of the faculties of the soul in the divine contemplation, the moving and trembling of the earth is the painful purgation of which it is the cause. To say that the way of God, by which the soul draws near unto Him, is in the sea, and His path in many waters, and therefore not known, is to say that this way to God is as secret, and as hidden from the senses of the soul, as the way of one who walks on the waters is from the senses of the body, and whose paths and steps are not known. The paths and steps of God in these souls which He is drawing to Himself, making them great in the union of His wisdom, have this property, that they are not known. That is the meaning of these words in the book of Job, impressing upon us this truth, 'Knowest thou the great paths of the clouds, and perfect knowledges?' that is, the paths and ways of God, in which He makes souls great and perfect in His wisdom; these are the clouds. This contemplation, therefore, which guides the soul to God is secret wisdom.

Chapter XVIII

Shows how this secret wisdom is also a ladder

1. The ladder by which to ascend to God.
2. And to descend to self by humility.
3. Vicissitudes of the spiritual life.
4. The ladder of Jacob's dream.
5. Science of love.

It remains for me to explain the second property, namely, how this secret wisdom is also a ladder. There are many reasons for calling secret contemplation a ladder. In the first place, as men employ ladders to mount up to those strong places where treasures are laid up, so also by secret contemplation, without knowing how, the soul ascends, and mounts upwards, to the knowledge and possession of the goods and treasures of heaven. This is well expressed by the royal prophet David when he says, 'Blessed is the man whose help is from Thee: he hath disposed ascensions in his heart, in the vale of tears, in the place which he hath appointed. For the Lawgiver shall give blessing; they shall go from virtue into virtue: the God of gods shall be seen in Sion.' He is the treasure of the citadel of Sion which is blessedness.

2. We may also call it a ladder, for as the steps of one and the same ladder serve to descend as well as to ascend by, so, too, those very communications which the soul receives in secret contemplation raise it up to God and make it humble. For the communications which really come from God have this property: they humble and exalt the soul at one and the same time. In the spiritual way, to

descend is to ascend, and to ascend is to descend, 'because every one that exalteth himself shall be humbled, and he that humbleth himself shall be exalted.' Moreover, as the virtue of humility is an exaltation, for the trial of the soul therein, God is wont to make it ascend by this ladder that it may descend, and make it descend that it may ascend; for thus are fulfilled the words of the Wise Man, 'Before he be broken the heart of a man is exalted, and before he be glorified it is humbled.'

3. If the soul will reflect on this from the natural point of view – I omit the spiritual which is not perceptible – it will easily see how uneven is the road; how after prosperity, which makes it glad, storms and trials follow at once, so that its previous repose seems to have been given it to prepare it and strengthen it for its present sufferings; how also, after misery and distress, come abundance and ease, so that the soul shall seem to have kept a vigil before the feast. This is the ordinary course of the state of contemplation, for until the soul attains to repose it never continues in one state; for all is ascending and descending. The reason is this; the state of perfection, which consists in the perfect love of God and contempt of self, can only subsist on two conditions, the knowledge of God and of oneself. The soul, therefore, must of necessity be tried in the one and the other, in the first which exalts it, by giving it to taste the sweetness of God, in the second which, by trials, humbles it, until, perfect habits having been acquired, it ceases to ascend and descend, having arrived at the summit, united with God, Who is at the top of it, and on Whom, too, the ladder rests.

4. The ladder of contemplation, which, as I have said, comes down from God, is shadowed forth by that ladder which Jacob saw in a dream, and the angels ascending and descending by it, from God to man and from man to God, Who was Himself leaning upon it. This took place by night, when Jacob slept, as the Scriptures declare, that we may learn from it how secret is the way and ascent unto God, and how different from all human conception. This is plain enough, for, in general, that which is to our greater profit – the loss and annihilation of self – we esteem a calamity; and that which is of but little

value – comfort and sweetness, where, in general, we lose instead of gaining – we look upon as the more advantageous for us.

5. But, to speak with more accuracy, and to the purpose, of the ladder of secret contemplation, I must observe that the chief reason why it is called a ladder is, that contemplation is the science of love, which is an infused loving knowledge of God, and which enlightens the soul and at the same time kindles within it the fire of love till it shall ascend upwards step by step unto God its Creator; for it is love only that unites the soul and God. With a view to the greater clearness of this matter, I shall mark the steps of this divine ladder, explaining concisely the signs and effects of each, that the soul may be able to form some conjecture on which of them it stands. I shall distinguish between them by their effects with St Bernard and St Thomas, and because it is not naturally possible to know them as they are in themselves, because the ladder of love is so secret that it can be weighed and measured by God only.

CHAPTER XIX

Begins the explanation of the ten degrees of the mystic ladder according to St Bernard and St Thomas

1. First step: the languishing of love.
2. The sick man.
3. Second step: the search for God.
4. Third step: good works.
5. Charity is not puffed up.
6. Fourth step: suffering without weariness.
7. The spirit regardless of the flesh.
8. Disinterested love.
9. Text.
10. Fifth step: the soul panteth after God.

The steps of the ladder of love, by which the soul, ascending from one to another, rises upwards to God, we say are ten. The first degree of love makes the soul languish to its great profit. On this the bride is speaking when she says, 'I adjure you, O daughters of Jerusalem, if you find my beloved, that you tell him that I languish with love.' This languishing is not unto death, but to the glory of God; for the soul here faints away as to sin and all things whatsoever that are not God, for God's sake, as the Psalmist testifies, saying: 'My spirit hath fainted away' from all things after Thy salvation; as he says in another place: 'My soul hath fainted after Thy salvation.'

2. As a sick man loses the desire for, and the taste of all food, and the colour vanishes from his face, so the soul in this degree of love loses all pleasure in earthly things, and all desire of them, and, like

one in love, changes its colour, that is, the conditions of the past life. The soul does not fall into this languishing state if the vehement heat descends not into it from above, which is the mystic fever, according to the words of the Psalmist, 'Voluntary rain shalt Thou separate, O God, to thine inheritance, and it was weakened, but Thou hast perfected it.' This languishing and fainting away as to all things – it is the first and earliest step to God – I have already explained, when I spoke of that annihilation to which the soul is brought when it begins to stand upon the ladder of contemplative purgation, when it finds no comfort, pleasure, nor support anywhere. In consequence of which it begins immediately to climb the second step of the ladder.

3. On the second step the soul is unremitting in its search after God. Thus the bride speaks of her seeking Him in her bed by night – she had fainted away when on the first step of the ladder – and not having found Him, says: 'I will rise; I will seek Him whom my soul loveth.' This is now the unceasing occupation of the soul. 'Seek ye the Lord, seek His face evermore,' is the counsel of the Psalmist, and never rest until He be found; like the bride who, when she had questioned the watchmen, passed on in her search, and left them. Mary Magdalene did not remain even with the angels at the sepulchre. So anxious is the soul now that it seeks the Beloved in all things; all its thoughts, words, and works are referred to Him; in eating, sleeping, and waking, all its anxieties are about Him, as I have already described it when speaking of the anxieties of love. As love becomes strong, regaining health, it commences the ascent to the third step by a new purgation in the night – as I shall hereafter explain – and which issues in the effects that follow.

4. The third step of the ladder of love renders the soul active and fervent, so that it faints not. Of this step the royal prophet said, 'Blessed is the man that feareth the Lord, he shall delight exceedingly in His commandments.' If then fear, being the fruit of love, produces this delight, what will be the effect of love itself? On this step the soul looks on great things as little, on many as few, its long service as short, by reason of the fire of love which is burning. It is with the soul as it was with Jacob, who 'served seven years for

Rachel, and they seemed but a few days, because of the greatness of his love.' If the love of a created being did so much in Jacob, what will the love of the Creator Himself do, when it shall have taken possession of the soul on the third step of the ladder?

5. Here the soul, because of the great love it has for God, is in great pain and suffering because of the scantiness of its service; if it could lawfully die for Him a thousand times it would be comforted. It looks upon itself therefore as unprofitable in all it does, and on its life as worthless. Another most wonderful effect is that it looks upon itself as being in truth the very worst of all, because its love continues to show it what is due to God; and then, because as it labours much in the service of God and sees how faulty and imperfect are its works, it is ashamed and distressed, seeing that the service it renders to God, Who is so high, is so exceedingly mean. On this third step the soul is very far from giving way to vainglory or presumption, or from condemning others. These anxious effects and others of the same kind are wrought in the soul when on the third step of the ladder, and so the soul acquires strength and courage to ascend to the fourth.

6. When the soul is on the fourth step of the ladder of love, it falls into a state of suffering, but without weariness, on account of the Beloved; for, as St Augustine saith, love makes all that is grievous and heavy to be light as nothing. It was on this step that the bride stood when, longing for the last, she said: 'Put me as a seal upon Thy heart, as a seal upon Thy arm; for love' – that is, the acts and operations of love – 'is strong as death; jealousy is hard as hell'.

7. The spirit is now so strong, and has so subdued the flesh, and makes so little of it, that it is as regardless of it as a tree of one of its leaves. It seeks not for consolation or sweetness either in God or elsewhere neither does it pray for God's gifts, seeing clearly how many it has already received. For all it cares for now is how it shall please God, and serve Him in some measure in return for His goodness, and for the graces it has received, and this at any and every cost.

8. It is now saying with heart and mind, my God and my Lord, how many there are who seek their own comfort and joy in Thee and

who pray for gifts and graces, but those who strive to please Thee, who offer Thee that which costs them something, and who cast their own interests aside, are very few; it is not Thy will to show mercy that fails, O my God! but it is we who fail in using Thy mercies in Thy service, so as to bind Thee to show us Thy mercy continually.

9. This degree of love is exceedingly high, for now as the soul, earnest in its love, always follows after God in the spirit of suffering for His sake, God frequently and, as it were, continually gives it joy, visiting it sweetly in spirit, for the boundless love of Christ, the Word, cannot look on the sufferings of the souls that love without coming to their relief. He has promised this by the mouth of the prophet Jeremias, saying, 'I have remembered thee, pitying thy youth . . . when thou followedst Me in the desert,' which in its spiritual sense is that detachment of the soul from all created things, not resting upon them nor at ease among them. On this fourth step of the ladder the soul is so inflamed with love, and so set on fire with the desire after God, that it ascends upwards to the fifth, which is the next.

10. On the fifth step of the ladder the soul longs after God, and desires Him with impatience. So great is the eagerness of the soul on this step to embrace, and be united to, the Beloved, that all delay, how slight soever, seems to it long, tedious, and oppressive, and it is ever thinking that it has found its love; but when it sees that its desires are disappointed – which is almost continually the case – it faints away through its longing, as the Psalmist says, speaking of this step: 'My soul longeth and fainteth for the courts of our Lord.' On this step the soul must either obtain its desires or die, as Rachel, because of her great longing for children, said to Jacob, her husband, 'Give me children, otherwise I shall die.' 'They suffer hunger like dogs and go round about the city.' In this degree of hunger the soul is now nourished by love, for as was its hunger so is its abundance, and so it ascends to the sixth step, the effects of which are as follows.

CHAPTER XX

Of the other five degrees

1. Sixth step: running in the way of God's commandments.
2. Seventh step: holy boldness in prayer.
3. Humility essential to every step of the ladder.
4. Eighth step: the possession of God.
5. Ninth step, the sweet fire of divine love.
6. Tenth step: the beatific vision.
7. Love reveals all secrets.

When the soul has ascended to the sixth step, it runs swiftly to God from Whom it receives many touches; and hope too runs without fainting, for love that has made it strong makes it fly rapidly. Of this step also Isaias speaks, saying: 'They that hope in our Lord shall change their strength, they shall take wings as eagles, they shall run and not labour, they shall walk and not faint.' To this step also the Psalmist refers: 'As the hart panteth after the fountains of waters, so my soul panteth after Thee, O God.' The hart when thirsty, runs very swiftly to the water. The cause of this swiftness which the soul experiences on this step is, that charity is enlarged, and the soul is now almost wholly purified, as it is written in the psalm: 'without iniquity have I run', and in another psalm, 'I ran the way of Thy commandments, when Thou didst dilate my heart', and thus the soul ascends immediately from the sixth to the seventh degree which follows.

2. On the seventh step the soul becomes vehemently bold, in this

intense and loving exaltation, no prudence can withhold it, no counsel control it, no shame restrain it; for the favour which God hath shown it has made it vehemently bold. This explains to us those words of the Apostle, that charity 'believeth all things, hopeth all things, endureth all things.' It was on this step that Moses spoke, when he said unto God: 'Either forgive them this trespass, or if Thou do not, strike me out of the book that Thou hast written.' Men of this spirit obtain from God what they so lovingly pray for. Hence the words of David: 'Delight in the Lord, and He will give thee the requests of thy heart.'

3. Standing on this step, the bride was bold, and said, 'Let Him kiss me with the kiss of His mouth.' But consider well here, it is not lawful to be thus bold, unless the soul feels that the interior favour of the King's sceptre is extended to it, lest it should fall down the steps already ascended; in all of which humility must ever be preserved. From this boldness and courage which God grants to the soul on the seventh step, that it may be bold with Him in the vehemence of its love, the soul ascends to the eighth, where it lays hold of the Beloved and is united to Him.

4. On the eighth step the soul embraces the Beloved and holds Him fast, according to the words of the bride: 'I found Him Whom my soul loveth; I held Him; and I will not let Him go.' On this step of union the desires of the soul are satisfied, but not without interruption. Some souls ascend to this step and at once fall back; if they did not, and remained there, they would have attained to a certain state of blessedness in this life, and thus the soul tarries but briefly on this step of the ladder. Daniel, being a man of desires, was bidden, on the part of God, to remain here: 'Daniel, thou man of desires, stand upright.' After this comes the ninth step, which is that of the perfect.

5. On the ninth step the soul is on fire sweetly. This step is that of the perfect who burn away sweetly in God, for this sweet and delicious burning is the work of the Holy Ghost because of the union of the soul with God. St Gregory says of the Apostles, that they burned interiorly with love sweetly, when the Holy Ghost descended upon them. The blessings and the riches of God which the soul now

enjoys cannot be described. And if we were to write many books on the subject there would still be more to say. For this reason, and because I intend to speak of it hereafter, I shall now say no more of this step, except that it is immediately followed by the tenth and the last, which does not belong to this life.

6. On the tenth step of the ladder the soul becomes wholly assimilated unto God in the beatific vision which it then immediately enjoys; for having ascended in this life to the ninth, it goeth forth out of the body. For these – they are few – being perfectly purified by love, do not pass through purgatory. For according to St Matthew, 'Blessed are the clean in heart, for they shall see God.' As I have said, the vision is the cause of the soul's perfect likeness unto God. 'We know', saith St John, 'that, when He shall appear, we shall be like to Him, because we shall see Him as He is. Not that the soul shall be as great as God, for that is not possible, but inasmuch as the soul is capable of it, it will be like unto God, and so is called, and is, by participation, God.

7. This is the secret ladder of which the soul speaks, though in the higher steps no longer secret, for love reveals itself exceedingly in the great effects it produces. But on the highest step, the beatific vision, the last of the ladder, where God is leaning, as I said before, nothing remains secret from the soul, by reason of its perfect likeness. And, therefore, our Saviour saith, 'In that day you shall not ask me anything.' Until that day come, notwithstanding the heights to which the soul ascends, something still remains secret from it, and that in proportion to the distance from its perfect likeness to the Divine Essence. In this way, then, by means of mystical theology and secret love, the soul goeth forth from all things and from itself, ascending upwards unto God. For love is like fire, which ever ascends, hastening to be absorbed in the centre of its sphere.

CHAPTER XXI

The meaning of 'disguised'. The colours in which the soul disguises itself in this night

1. The disguise.
2. Why it is necessary.
3. Three colours, white, green, and purple.
4. Faith the breastplate of defence against the devil.
5. Inner garment of faith.
6. When and how assumed.
7. Hope the helmet of protection against the world.
8. Description of the helmet.
9. The soul by hope obtains its desires.
10. The royal robe of charity shields the soul from the flesh.
11. The intellect vested in faith, the memory in hope.
12. The will in charity.

Having now explained why contemplation is called a secret ladder, I have further to explain what is meant by the word 'disguised'; for the soul says that it went forth by the secret ladder 'disguised'.

2. For the understanding of the whole matter it is necessary to keep in mind that to be disguised is nothing else but to hide oneself under another form than our own, either for the purpose of showing under that concealment the will and purpose of the heart with a view to gain the goodwill and affection of the person beloved, or for the purpose of escaping the observation of rivals, and thereby the better effect our object. Such a person assumes the disguise which shall

most represent and manifest the affection of his heart, and which shall the best conceal him from his rivals.

3. The soul, then, touched with the love of its Bridegroom Christ, that it may gain His favour and goodwill, sallies forth in that disguise which shall most vividly represent the affections of the mind and secure it against the assaults of its enemies, the devil, the world, and the flesh. The disguise it assumes is, therefore, a garment of three principal colours, white, green, and purple, emblems of the three theological virtues, faith, hope, and charity; by the help of which it shall not only enter into the good graces of the Beloved, but shall also be most secure and protected against its three enemies.

4. The faith is a garment of such surpassing whiteness as to dazzle the eyes of every understanding; for when the soul has put on faith it becomes invisible and inaccessible to the devil, because it is then most securely defended against him – better even than by the other virtues, – its strongest and most cunning foe.

5. St Peter knew of no better defence against the devil than faith, for he said, 'whom resist, steadfast in faith'. And with a view of entering into favour and union with the Beloved, the soul cannot put on a better garment, as the ground of the other virtues, than the white tunic of faith, for without it, the Apostle saith, 'It is impossible to please God.' But with a living faith the soul cannot but be pleasing and acceptable unto God, for He says so Himself by the mouth of the prophet: 'I will espouse thee to Me in faith.' It is as if He said to the soul, If thou wilt be united and betrothed to Me, thou must draw near inwardly clad in faith.

6. The soul put on the white robe of faith on its going forth on this dark night, when walking in the darkness amidst interior trials, as I said before, it received no ray of light from the understanding; not from above, because heaven seemed shut and God hidden; not from below, because its spiritual directors gave it no comfort. It bore its trials patiently and persevered, without fainting or falling away from the Beloved, Who by these crosses and tribulations tried the faith of His bride, that it might be able hereafter truly to say with the Psalmist, 'For the words of Thy lips, I have kept hard ways.'

7. Over the white robe of faith the soul puts on forthwith that of the second colour, a green coat, emblem of the virtue of hope, by which it is delivered and protected from its second enemy, the world. The freshness of a living hope in God fills the soul with such energy and resolution, with such aspirations after the things of eternal life, that all this world seems to it – as indeed it is – in comparison with that which it hopes for, dry, withered, dead, and worthless. The soul now denudes itself of the garments and trappings of the world, by setting the heart upon nothing that is in it, and hoping for nothing that is, or may be, in it, living only in the hope of everlasting life. And, therefore, when the heart is thus lifted up above the world, the world cannot touch it or lay hold of it, nor even see it.

8. The soul then, thus disguised and clad in the vesture of hope, is secure from its second foe, the world, for St Paul calls hope the helmet of salvation. Now a helmet is armour which protects and covers the whole head, and has no opening except in one place, where the eyes may look through. Hope is such a helmet, for it covers all the senses of the head of the soul in such a way that they cannot be lost in worldly things, and leaves no part of them exposed to the arrows of the world. It has one loophole only through which the eyes may look upwards only; this is the ordinary work of hope, to direct the eyes of the soul to God alone; as David saith, 'My eyes are always to our Lord', looking for succour nowhere else; as he saith in another psalm, 'As the eyes of the handmaid on the hands of her mistress, so are our eyes to our Lord God until He have mercy on us,' hoping in Him.

9. The green vesture of hope – for the soul is then ever looking upwards unto God, disregarding all else, and delighting only in Him – is so pleasing to the Beloved that the soul obtains from Him all it hopes for. This is why He tells the soul in the Canticle, 'Thou hast wounded My heart in one of thine eyes.' It would have been useless for the soul, if it had not put on the green robe of hope in God, to claim such love, for it would not have succeeded, because that which influences the Beloved, and prevails, is persevering hope. It is in the

vesture of hope that the soul goes forth disguised in this secret and dark night; seeing that it goes forth so detached from all possession, without any consolations, that it regards nothing, and that its sole anxiety is about God, putting its 'mouth in the dust if so be there may be hope,' in the words of Jeremias quoted already.

10. Over the white and green robes, as the crown and perfection of its disguise, the soul puts on the third, the splendid robe of purple. This is the emblem of charity, which not only enhances the beauty of the others, but which so elevates the soul and renders it so lovely and pleasing in His eyes that it ventures to say to Him, 'I am black but beautiful, O daughters of Jerusalem, therefore hath the king loved me and brought me into His secret chamber.' This robe of charity, which is that of love, not only defends and protects the soul from its third enemy, the flesh – for where the true love of God is there is no room for self-love or for selfishness – but strengthens the other virtues also, and makes them flourish for the protection of the soul, beautifying it and adorning it with grace, so that it shall please the Beloved; for without charity no virtue is pleasing unto God. This is the purple, spoken of in the Canticle, by which the soul ascends to the seat where God reposes: 'the seat of gold, the going up of purple.' It is vested in this robe of purple that the soul journeys, as the first stanza declares, when in the dark night it went out of itself, and from all created things, with anxious love inflamed, by the secret ladder of contemplation to the perfect union of the love of God its beloved Saviour.

11. This, then, is that disguise which the soul says it puts on in the night of faith on the secret ladder; and these are the three colours of it, namely, a certain most fitting disposition for its union with God in its three powers, memory, understanding, and will. Faith blinds the understanding, and empties it of all natural intelligence, and thereby disposes it for union with the divine wisdom. Hope empties the memory and withdraws it from all created things which can possess it; for as St Paul saith, 'Hope that is seen is not hope.' Thus the memory is withdrawn from all things on which it might dwell in this life, and is fixed on what the soul hopes to possess. Hope in God

alone, therefore, purely disposes the memory according to the measure of the emptiness it has wrought for union with Him.

12. Charity in the same way empties the affections and desires of the will of everything that is not God, and fixes them on Him alone. This virtue of charity, then, disposes the will and unites it with God in love. And because these virtues – it being their special work – withdraw the soul from all that is not God, so also do they serve to unite the soul to Him. It is impossible for the soul to attain to the perfection of the love of God unless it journeys, in earnest, in the robes of these three virtues. This disguise, therefore, which the soul assumed when it went forth in order to obtain that which it aimed at, the loving and delightful union with the Beloved, was most necessary and expedient. And it was also a great happiness to have succeeded in thus disguising itself and persevering in it until it obtained the desired end, the union of love, as it declares in the next line.

CHAPTER XXII

Explains the third line of the second stanza

Happiness of the soul in having overcome its enemies.

O happy lot!

It is very evident that it was a blessed thing for the soul to have succeeded in such an enterprise as this, by which it was delivered out of the hands of Satan, from the world, and from its own sensuality, in which, having gained that liberty of spirit so precious and desirable, it rose from meanness to dignity, from being earthly and human became heavenly and divine, having its 'conversation in Heaven', like unto those who are in a state of perfection, as I shall proceed to explain.

2. I shall, however, be brief, because the most important point – that which chiefly determined me to explain this dark night to many souls who enter on it without knowing it, as I said in the preface – has been already in some degree explained, and I have also shown, though not in adequate terms, how great are the blessings that descend upon the soul in this night, and what a great happiness it is to be passing through it. This I did that when such souls are alarmed at the trials that have come upon them, they may be encouraged by the certain hope of the numerous and great blessings of God which they receive in this night. Besides this, it was a happy lot for the soul for the reason assigned in the following line.

CHAPTER XXIII

Explains the fourth line – describes the wonderful hiding-place of the soul in this night, and how the devil, though he enters other most secret places, enters not this

1. Explanation.
2. Darkness and concealment.
3. Sense should be ignorant of what happens in the spirit.
4. The devil ascertains the state of the spirit by evidences of the sensitive nature.
5. The spiritual assaults of Satan.
6. Spirit against spirit.
7. The soul the prize of a contest.
8. Moses and the magicians of Egypt.
9. Satan cannot imitate spiritual visions.
10. God suffers the devil to afflict the soul.
11. Neither angel nor devil can penetrate the soul directly.
12. Continuation.
13. Continuation.
14. The soul conscious of two forces.
15. Conclusion.

In darkness and concealment,

'In concealment,' that is, secretly or hidden. So when the soul says that it went forth in darkness and concealment, it explains more clearly the great safety spoken of in the first line of this stanza –

which it finds in this dim contemplation on the road of the union of the love of God.

2. The words of the soul 'darkness and concealment' mean here that the soul, because it went forth in the dark, travelled in secret, undiscovered by the evil one, beyond the reach of his wiles and stratagems. The reason why the soul is free, concealed from the devil and his wiles in the dimness of this contemplation, is, that infused contemplation, to which it is now admitted, is passively infused into it, in secret, without the cognizance of the senses, and of the interior and exterior powers of the sensual part. And that, too, is the reason why it escapes, not only from the embarrassments which the faculties, and naturally, through their weakness, present before it, but also from the evil one, who, were it not for the sensual faculties, could never know what is passing in the soul. The more spiritual therefore the communication is, and the further it is removed beyond the reach of sense, the less able is the devil to perceive it.

3. This being so, it greatly concerns the soul's security, that the lower senses should be in the dark, and have no knowledge of the interior conversation of the soul with God, and that for two reasons; first, that the spiritual communication may be the more abundant, for then the weakness of the sensual part hinders not liberty of spirit. The second is, that the soul is more secure because the evil one cannot know what is passing within it. The words of our Lord, 'Let not thy left hand know what thy right hand doth,' may be, in a spiritual sense, understood of this, and we may understand Him to say: Let not thy left hand, that is man's lower nature, know what is passing in the higher and spiritual part of the soul. That is, let the divine communications remain unknown to the lower senses, and a secret between the spirit and God.

4. It is very true, that oftentimes when these interior and most secret spiritual communications are made to the soul, the devil, though he knows neither their nature nor their form, ascertains their presence, and that the soul is then receiving some great blessings, merely from observing the silence and repose some of them effect in the senses, and in the powers of our lower nature. And then, when he

sees that he cannot thwart them in the inmost depth of the soul, he does all he can to disquiet and disturb the sensual part which is accessible to him, now by pain and at another time by horrible dread, intending thereby to trouble the higher and spiritual part of the soul, and to frustrate the blessings it then receives and enjoys.

5. But very often when this contemplation pours its light purely into the spirit and exerts its strength therein, the devil, with all his efforts, is not able to disturb it, for then the soul becomes the recipient of renewed benefits, love, and a more secure peace; for, wonderful to tell! in its consciousness of the disturbing presence of the foe, it enters deeply into itself, without knowing how it comes to pass and without any action on its own part, and feels assured of a certain refuge where it can hide itself beyond the reach of the evil one; and thus its peace and joy are increased, of which the devil attempted to rob it. All those terrors assail it only from without; it sees clearly, and exults, that it can in the meanwhile securely enjoy in secret the calm peace and sweetness of the Bridegroom, which the world and the devil can neither give nor take away. The soul is now experiencing the truth of that which the bride says in the Canticle, 'Behold, threescore valiants . . . compass the bed of Solomon . . . for fears by night.' Strength and peace abound within the soul, though it feels the flesh and the bones frequently tormented without.

6. At other times, when the spiritual communications flow over into the senses, the devil succeeds the more easily in disquieting the mind, and in disturbing it with the terrors with which he assails it through the senses. At that time the mental agonies are great, and occasionally surpassing all description; for when spirit has to do with spirit, the evil one causes an intolerable horror in the good one, that is, in the soul, when it succeeds in disturbing it. This is the meaning of the bride in her account of that which happened to her when she tried to be interiorly recollected, so as to have the fruition of these goods: 'I came down', she says, 'into the garden of nuts to see the fruits of the valleys, and to look if the vineyard had flourished. . . . I knew not; my soul troubled me for the chariots and the noise of Aminadab,' that is the devil.

7. This attack of the devil takes place also when God bestows His favours upon a soul by the instrumentality of a good angel; sometimes he even perceives the favours granted by God Himself, and ordinarily those bestowed on the soul through the instrumentality of a good angel become known to the enemy, that he may do what he can, according to the measure of justice, against that soul, and that he may be debarred from pleading that he had no opportunity of seizing on that soul as he did in the case of Job, which would be the case if God did not place these two combatants, the good angel and the devil, on an equality when they contend for the soul, in order that the victory may be of greater worth, and that the soul, triumphant and faithful in temptation, may be the more abundantly rewarded.

8. This is the reason – and it is right we should observe it – why God, in the order of grace and in just proportion to His own operation, permits Satan to disquiet and tempt the soul which He is guiding therein. When such a soul has real visions, through the instrumentality of an angel (this being the rule, whereas it hardly ever happens that Christ appears in His own person), God suffers the evil spirit to represent false visions of the same kind, in such a way that an incautious soul may be very easily deluded, as it has happened to many. We have an instance of this in Exodus, where we read that the magicians of Pharaoh wrought apparently signs and wonders resembling those really wrought by Moses. For when Moses brought forth frogs, the magicians of Egypt did the same; and when he turned water into blood, so did the magicians.

9. It is not in bodily visions only that the evil spirit apes God, but in spiritual communications also, which are effected through the instrumentality of an angel, whenever he succeeds in discovering them. For as Job saith, 'He seeth every high thing,' that is, he apes them, and insinuates himself among them as well as he can. Spiritual visions have neither form nor figure – that is the characteristic of spirit – and, therefore, Satan cannot imitate them, nor occasion others which shall in any way represent them. And so when the good angel communicates spiritual contemplation, the evil spirit, while

the soul is being thus visited, appears to it in order to attack and destroy one spiritual effect by another. When this happens at the time the good angel imparts to the soul the favour of contemplation, the latter cannot so swiftly hide itself in the secrecy of contemplation as not to be watched by Satan who presents himself before it with a certain horror and spiritual confusion, which is occasionally exceedingly painful. Sometimes the soul can quickly disembarrass itself, so that the terror of the evil spirit shall have no time to make any impression upon it, and recollects itself, favoured herein by that spiritual grace which the good angel then communicates.

10. Sometimes, too, the evil spirit prevails and infests the soul with this horror and trouble, and this is a greater torment to the soul than all the evils of this life can be; for this horrible communication goes straight from spirit to spirit, divested of all that is corporal, in a manner painful beyond all bodily suffering. This lasts some time in the spirit only, but not long, else the vehemence of the communication of the evil spirit would drive the soul from the body; but the remembrance of it is sufficient to produce great pain. All this passes in the soul without its doing or undoing anything of itself to bring about these representations or impressions. But we must remember that, when the good angel suffers the evil spirit thus to afflict the soul, it is with a view to purify and prepare it by that spiritual vigil for some great festival and spiritual grace which it is his will to bestow upon it, for he never mortifies but to give life, and never humbles but to exalt. This speedily ensues; for the soul, according to the measure of the dark purgation it has undergone, enters on the fruition of sweet spiritual contemplation, and that so sublime at times that no language can describe it. The horror of the evil spirit so refines the soul as to render it capable of so great a good, for these spiritual visions appertain to the next life rather than to this; and while one is being seen another is in preparation. This is to be understood of those visitations which God makes by the ministry of an angel, and wherein the soul, as I said before, is not wholly secure, nor in such darkness and concealment as to be altogether unobserved by the enemy.

11. But when God visits the soul Himself, the words of the stanza are then true, for, in perfect darkness hidden from the enemy, it receives, at such times, the spiritual graces of God. The reason of the difference is that God, being the sovereign Lord, dwells substantially in the soul, and that neither angel nor devil can discover what is going on there, nor penetrate the profound and secret communications which take place between Him and the soul. These communications, because the work of our Lord Himself, are wholly divine and supreme, and, as it were, substantial touches of the divine union between Himself and the soul; in one of these, because it is the highest possible degree of prayer, the soul receives greater good than in all the rest. These are the touches for which the bride in the Canticle prayed, saying, 'Let Him kiss me with the kiss of His mouth.'

12. This being a state so near unto God, into which the soul so anxiously longs to enter, one touch of the Godhead is prized and desired by it above all the other gifts which God grants it. For this reason the bride in the Canticle, after the great things wrought in her, of which she there sings, not finding them enough, prays for the divine touches, saying: 'Who shall give to me Thee my brother, sucking the breasts of my mother, that I may find thee without, and kiss Thee with the mouth of my soul, and now no man despise me, or presume to assail me.' These words relate to that communication which God makes alone, without, and hidden from all creatures; that is the meaning of the words 'alone', 'without', and 'sucking', drying up and causing to wither the breasts, that is the appetites and affections of the sensual part. This occurs when the soul in liberty of spirit enjoys these blessings in sweetness and inward peace, the sensual part thereof unable to hinder it, and the devil by means of it not able to disturb it.

13. Then indeed the evil spirit would not venture to assail the soul, because he could not succeed, neither can he know of those divine touches in the substance of the soul with the loving substance of God. No man can arrive at this blessed condition but by the most perfect purgation and detachment, by being spiritually hidden from

all created things. It is a work wrought in the dark (as has been fully explained above, and again with reference to this verse), in the hiding place, wherein the soul is confirmed more and more in union with God by love; and, therefore, the soul sings, 'In darkness and concealment'.

14. Sometimes when these favours are granted to the soul in secret, that is, in the spirit only, the higher and lower portions of the soul seem to it – it knows not how – to be so far apart that it recognizes two parts in itself, each so distant from the other that neither seems to have anything in common with the other, being in appearance so far removed and apart. And, in reality, this is in a certain manner true, for in its present operations, which are wholly spiritual, it has no commerce with the sensual part.

15. Thus the soul becomes wholly spiritual, and the spiritual passions and desires are in a high degree suppressed in this hiding place of unitive contemplation. The soul then, speaking of its higher part, sings the last line of this stanza, 'My house being now at rest.'

CHAPTER XXIV

Concludes the explanation of the second stanza

1. Explanation.
2. Twofold rest: the flesh at peace with the spirit, the spirit with God.
3. Divine espousals.
4. Continuation.

My house being now at rest.

This is as much as saying, My higher nature and my lower nature also, each in its desires and powers, being now at rest, I went forth to the divine union of the love of God.

2. As in the warfare of the dark night, as I said before, the soul undergoes a twofold contest and purgation: that is, in the sensual and the spiritual part, with their senses, powers, and passions, so also, in the sensual and spiritual parts, with all their powers and desires, does it attain to a twofold peace and rest. For this reason it repeats the words, as I said before, 'My house being now at rest,' at the end of the second stanza, because of the two parts of the soul, spiritual and sensual, which, if they are to go forth into the divine union of love, must first of all be changed, ordered, and tranquillized with regard to all the things of sense and spirit, after the likeness of the state of innocence in Adam, notwithstanding that the soul be not wholly delivered from the temptations of the lower part. These words, therefore, which in the first stanza are understood of the tranquillity of the lower and sensual part, now, in the second stanza,

are understood particularly of the higher and spiritual part; and this is the reason of the repetition.

3. The soul obtains this tranquillity and rest of the spiritual house, habitually and perfectly – so far as it is possible in this life – through the substantial touches of the divine union, of which I have just spoken, and which, in secret, hidden from the turmoil of Satan, sense, and passion, it receives from the Divinity, whereby it has been tranquillized, purified, strengthened, and confirmed, so as to become an effectual partaker of that union which is its divine betrothal to the Son of God. The instant the two houses of the soul are tranquil and confirmed, with the whole household of its powers and desires sunk in sleep and silence, as to all things of heaven and earth, the divine Wisdom, immediately in a new bond of loving possession, unites itself to the soul, and that is fulfilled which is written, 'While quiet silence contained all things and the night was in the mid-way of her course, Thy omnipotent Word sallying out of heaven from the royal seats.' The same truth is set before us in the Canticle, where the bride, after passing by those who took her veil away and wounded her, saith, 'When I had a little passed by them, I found Him whom my soul loveth.'

4. This union is unattainable without great purity, and this purity is attainable only by detachment from all created things and sharp mortifications. This is signified by the robbery of the veil and the wounding of the bride in the night when she went forth searching after her beloved; for the new veil of the betrothal cannot be put on till the old veil be taken away. He, therefore, who will not go out in this dark night to seek the Beloved, who will not deny and mortify his own will, but seek Him at his ease on his bed, as the bride once did, will never find Him. The soul says here that it found Him, as the soul says of itself that it found Him by going forth in the dark, and in the anxieties of love.

CHAPTER XXV

In which the third stanza is briefly explained

1. Explanation.
2. Blessings of the spiritual night.
3. Second blessing.
4. To suffer but not to die.

> *In that happy night,*
> *In secret, seen of none,*
> *Seeing nought myself,*
> *Without other light or guide*
> *Save that which in my heart was burning.*

The soul still continues the metaphor of natural night in celebrating and magnifying the blessings of the night of the spirit, by means of which it has been able quickly and securely to compass the desired end. Three of these blessings are set before us in this stanza.

2. The first is that in this blessed night of contemplation God is guiding the soul by a road so solitary and so secret, so remote and alien from sense, that nothing belonging thereto, nor any created thing, can approach it so as to disturb it or detain it on the road of the union of love.

3. The second blessing is that because of the spiritual darkness of this night, in which all the faculties of the higher part of the soul are in darkness, the soul, seeing nothing, and unable to see, is not detained by anything which is not God from drawing near unto Him, and, therefore, advances unhindered by forms and figures and

natural apprehensions: for these are the things which usually hinder the soul from being always in union with God.

4. The third blessing is, that though the soul is supported by no particular interior light of the understanding, nor by any exterior guide comforting it on this high road – the thick darkness has deprived it of all this – yet love and faith, now burning within it, drawing the heart towards the Beloved, influence and guide it, and make it fly upwards to God along the road of solitude, while it knows neither how nor by what means that is done.

> *In that happy night,*
> *In secret, seen of none,*
> *Seeing nought myself,*
> *Without other light or guide*
> *Save that which in my heart was burning.*

END OF THE DARK NIGHT

The Living Flame of Love

PROLOGUE

It is not without some unwillingness that, at the requests of others, I
enter upon the explanation of the four stanzas because they relate to
matters so interior and spiritual as to baffle the powers of language.
The spiritual transcends the sensual, and he speaks but indifferently
of the mind of the spirit who has not a spiritual mind himself. I have,
therefore, in consideration of my own defects, put off this matter
until now. But now that our Lord seems in some way to have opened
to me the way of knowledge herein, and to have given me some
fervour of spirit, I have resolved to enter on the subject. I know too
well that of myself I can say nothing to the purpose on any subject,
how much less then on a matter of such depth and substance as this!
What is mine here will be nothing but the defects and errors, and I
therefore submit the whole to the better judgment and discretion of
our Holy Mother the Catholic Roman Church, under whose guidance no one goeth astray. And now having said this, I will venture, in
reliance on the Holy Writings, to give utterance to what I may have
learned, observing at the same time, that all I say falls far short of
that which passes in this intimate union of the soul with God.

2. There is nothing strange in the fact that God bestows favours so
great and so wonderful upon those souls whom He is pleased to
comfort. For if we consider that it is God Himself as God, and with
infinite love and goodness, Who bestows them; and this being the case,
they will not seem unreasonable, for He hath said Himself that the
Father and the Son and the Holy Ghost will come to him that loves
Him, and will dwell in him. And this is accomplished in making such
an one live and abide in the Father, the Son, and the Holy Ghost, in
the life of God, as it shall be explained in the stanzas that follow.

3. In the former stanzas I spoke of the highest degree of perfection to which it is possible to attain in this life, transformation in God; yet these, the explanation of which I now propose to undertake, speak of that love still more perfect and complete in the same state of transformation. For though it is true that the former and the present stanzas refer to one and the same state of transformation, and that no soul can pass beyond it as such, still with time and habits of devotion, the soul is more perfected and grounded in it. Thus, when a log of wood is set on fire, and when it is transformed into fire and united with it, the longer it burns and the hotter the fire, the more it glows until sparks and flames are emitted from it.

4. So too the soul – and this is the subject of these stanzas – when transformed, and glowing interiorly in the fire of love, is not only united with the divine fire, but becomes a living flame, and itself conscious of it. The soul speaks of this with an intimate delicious sweetness of love, burning in its own flame, dwelling upon the various marvellous effects wrought within it. These effects I now proceed to describe, following the same method: that is, I shall first transcribe the four stanzas, then each separately, and finally each line by itself as I explain them.

STANZAS

I

O Living Flame of Love,
That woundest tenderly
My soul in its inmost depth!
As Thou art no longer grievous,
Perfect Thy work, if it be Thy will,
Break the web of this sweet encounter.

II

O sweet burn!
O delicious wound!

O tender hand! O gentle touch!
Savouring of everlasting life,
And paying the whole debt,
By slaying Thou hast changed death into life.

III

O lamps of fire,
In the splendours of which
The deep caverns of sense,
Dim and dark,
With unwonted brightness
Give light and warmth together to their Beloved!

IV

How gently and how lovingly
Thou wakest in my bosom,
Where alone Thou secretly dwellest;
And in Thy sweet breathing
Full of grace and glory,
How tenderly Thou fillest me with Thy love.

EXPLANATION OF THE FIRST STANZA

The bride of Christ, now feeling herself to be all on fire in the divine union, and that rivers of living waters are flowing from her belly, as Christ our Lord said they would flow from the like souls, believes that, as she is transformed in God with such vehemence and so intimately possessed by Him, so richly adorned with gifts and graces, she is near unto bliss, and that a slender veil only separates her from it. Seeing, too, that this sweet flame of love burning within her, each time it touches her, makes her as it were glorious with foretaste of glory, so much so that whenever it absorbs and assails her, it seems to be admitting her to everlasting life, and to rend the veil of her mortality, she addresses herself, with a great longing, to the flame, which is the Holy Ghost, and prays Him to destroy her mortal life in this sweet encounter, and bestow upon her in reality what He seems about to give, namely, perfect glory, crying: 'O living flame of love.'

O living flame of love,

2. In order to express the fervour and reverence with which the soul is speaking in these four stanzas, it begins them with 'O' and 'How', which are significant of great earnestness, and whenever uttered show that something passes within that is deeper than the tongue can tell. 'O' is the cry of strong desire, and of earnest supplication, in the way of persuasion. The soul employs it in both senses here, for it magnifies and intimates its great desire, calling upon love to end its mortal life.

3. This flame of love is the Spirit of the Bridegroom, the Holy Ghost, of whose presence within itself the soul is conscious, not only as fire which consumes it, and transforms it in sweet love, but as a fire burning within it, sending forth a flame which bathes it in glory and recreates it with the refreshment of everlasting life. The work of the Holy Ghost in a soul transformed in His love is this: His interior action within it is to kindle it and set it on fire; this is the burning of love, in union with which the will loves most deeply, being now one by love with that flame of fire. And thus the soul's acts of love are most precious, and even one of them more meritorious than many elicited not in the state of transformation. The transformation in love differs from the flame of love as a habit differs from an act, or as the glowing fuel from the flames it emits, the flames being the effect of the fire which is there burning.

4. Hence then we may say of the soul which is transformed in love, that its ordinary state is that of the fuel in the midst of the fire; that the acts of such a soul are the flames which rise up out of the fire of love, vehement in proportion to the intensity of the fire of union, and to the rapture and absorption of the will in the flame of the Holy Ghost; rising like the angel who ascended to God in the flame which consumed the holocaust of Manue. And as the soul, in its present

condition, cannot elicit these acts without a special inspiration of the Holy Ghost, all these acts must be divine, in so far as the soul is under the special influence of God. Hence then it seems to the soul, as often as the flame breaks forth, causing it to love sweetly with a heavenly disposition, that its life everlasting is begun, and that its acts are divine in God.

5. This is the language in which God addresses purified and stainless souls, namely, words of fire. 'Thy word,' saith the Psalmist, 'is a vehement fire.' And in Jeremias we read, 'are not My words as a fire? saith our Lord.' His 'words', we learn from Himself, 'are spirit and life'; the power and efficacy of which are felt by such souls as have ears to hear; pure souls full of love. But those souls whose palate is not healthy, whose desire is after other things, cannot perceive the spirit and life of His words. And therefore the more wonderful the words of the Son of God, the more insipid they are to some who hear them, because of the impurity in which they live.

6. Thus, when He announced the doctrine of the Holy Eucharist, a doctrine full of sweetness and of love, 'many of His disciples went back.' If such persons as these have no taste for the words of God which He speaks inwardly to them, it is not to be supposed that all others are like them. St Peter loved the words of Christ, for he replied, 'Lord, to whom shall we go? Thou hast the words of eternal life.' The woman of Samaria forgot the water, and 'left her waterpot' at the well, because of the sweetness of the words of God.

7. And now when the soul has drawn so near unto God as to be transformed in the flame of love, when the Father and the Son and the Holy Ghost are in communion with it, is it anything incredible to say that it has a foretaste – though not perfectly, because this life admits not of it – of everlasting life in this fire of the Holy Ghost? This is the reason why this flame is said to be a *living* flame, not because it is not always living, but because its effect is to make the soul live spiritually in God, and to be conscious of such a life, as it is written, 'My heart and my flesh have rejoiced toward the living God.' The Psalmist makes use of the word 'living', not because it was necessary, for God is ever-living, but to show that the body and

the spirit had a lively feeling of God; that is the rejoicing in the living God. Thus, in this flame, the soul has so vivid a sense of God, and a perception of Him so sweet and delicious, that it cries out: 'O living flame of love!'

That woundest tenderly

8. That is, Thou touchest me tenderly in Thy love. For when this flame of divine life wounds the soul with the gentle languishing for the life of God, it wounds it with so much endearing tenderness, and softens it so that it melts away in love. The words of the bride in the Canticle are now fulfilled in the soul. 'My soul melted when He spoke.' This is the effect in the soul when God speaks.

9. But how can we say that it wounds the soul, when there is nothing to wound, seeing that it is all consumed in the fire of love? It is certainly marvellous; for as fire is never idle, but in continual movement, flashing in one direction, then in another, so love, the function of which is to wound, so as to cause love and joy, when it exists in the soul as a living flame, darts forth its most tender flames of love, causing wounds, exerting joyously all the arts and wiles of love as in the palace of its wedding feast. So Assuerus exhibited his riches, and the glory of his power at 'the wedding and marriage of Esther'; and so is wrought in the soul what is read in the Proverbs: I 'was delighted every day . . . playing in the world, and My delights were to be with the children of men,' that is to give Myself to them. This wounding, therefore, which is the 'playing' of divine wisdom, is the flames of those tender touches which touch the soul continually, touches of the fire of love which is never idle. And of these flashings of the fire it is said that they wound the soul in its inmost substance.

My soul in its inmost depth!

10. The feast of the Holy Ghost is celebrated in the substance of the soul, which is inaccessible to the devil, the world, and the flesh; and therefore the more interior the feast, the more secure, substantial, and delicious is it. For the more interior it is, the purer it is; and the greater the purity, the greater the abundance, frequency, and

universality of God's communication of Himself; and thus the joy of the soul and spirit is so much the greater, for it is God Himself Who is the author of all this, and the soul doeth nothing of itself, in the sense I shall immediately explain.

11. And inasmuch as the soul cannot work naturally here, nor make any efforts of its own otherwise than through the bodily senses and by their help – of which it is in this case completely free, and from which it is most detached – the work of the soul is solely to receive what God communicates, who alone in the depths of the soul, without the help of the senses, can influence and direct it, and operate within it. Thus, then, all the movements of such a soul are divine, and though of God, still they are the soul's, because God effects them within it, itself willing them and assenting to them.

12. The expression, 'inmost depth', implies other depths of the soul less profound, and it is necessary to consider this. In the first place the soul, regarded as spirit, has neither height nor depth of greater or less degree in its own nature, as bodies have which have bulk. The soul has no parts, neither is there any difference between its interior and exterior, for it is uniform; it has no depths of greater or less profundity, nor can one part of it be more enlightened than another, as is the case with physical bodies, for the whole of it is enlightened uniformly at once.

13. Setting aside this signification of depth, material and measureable, we say that the inmost depth of the soul is there where its being, power, and the force of its action and movement penetrate and cannot go further. Thus fire, or a stone, tend by their natural force to the centre of their sphere, and cannot go beyond it, or help resting there, unless some obstacle intervene. Accordingly, when a stone lies on the ground it is said to be within its centre, because within the sphere of its active motion, which is the element of earth, but not in the inmost depth of that centre, the middle of the earth, because it has still power and force to descend thither, provided all that hinders it be taken away. So when it shall have reached the centre of the earth, and is incapable of further motion of its own, we say of it that it is then in its inmost or deepest centre.

14. The centre of the soul is God. When the soul shall have reached Him, according to its essence, and according to the power of its operations, it will then have attained to its ultimate and deepest centre in God. This will be when the soul shall love Him, comprehend Him, and enjoy Him with all its strength. When, however, the soul has not attained to this state, though it be in God, Who is the centre of it by grace and communion with Him, still if it can move further and is not satisfied, though in the centre, it is not in the deepest centre, because there is still room for it to advance.

15. Love unites the soul with God, and the greater its love the deeper does it enter into God, and the more is it centred in Him. According to this way of speaking we may say, that as the degrees of love, so are the centres which the soul finds in God. These are the many mansions of the Father's house. Thus, a soul which has but one degree of love is already in God, Who is its centre: for one degree of love is sufficient for our abiding in Him in the state of grace. If we have two degrees of love we shall then have found another centre, more interiorly in God; and if we have three we shall have reached another and more interior centre still.

16. But if the soul shall have attained to the highest degree of love, the love of God will then wound it in its inmost depth or centre; and the soul will be transformed and enlightened in the highest degree in its substance, faculties, and strength, until it shall become most like unto God. The soul in this state may be compared to crystal, lucid and pure; the greater the light thrown upon it, the more luminous it becomes by the concentration thereof, until at last it seems to be all light and undistinguishable from it; it being then so illumined, and to the utmost extent, that it seems to be one with the light itself.

17. The flame wounds the soul in its inmost depth; that is, it wounds it when it touches the very depths of its substance, power and force. This expression implies that abundance of joy and bliss, which is the greater and the more tender, the more vehemently and substantially the soul is transformed and centred in God. It greatly surpasses that which occurs in the ordinary union of love, for it is in

proportion to the greater heat of the fire of love which now emits the living flame. The soul which has the fruition only of the ordinary union of love may be compared, in a certain sense, to the 'fire' of God which is in Sion, that is in the Church Militant; while the soul which has the fruition of glory so sweet may be compared to 'His furnace in Jerusalem', which means the vision of peace.

18. The soul in the burning furnace is in a more peaceful, glorious, and tender union, the more the flame of the furnace transcends the fire of ordinary love. Thus the soul, feeling that the living flame ministers to it all good – divine love brings all blessings with it – cries out: 'O living flame of love, that woundest tenderly.' The cry of the soul is: O kindling burning love, how tenderly dost thou make me glorious by thy loving movements in my greatest power and strength, giving me a divine intelligence according to the capacity of my understanding, and communicating love according to the utmost freedom of my will; that is, thou hast elevated to the greatest height, by the divine intelligence, the powers of my understanding in the most intense fervour and substantial union of my will. This ineffable effect then takes place when this flame of fire rushes upwards in the soul. The divine wisdom absorbs the soul – which is now purified and most clean – profoundly and sublimely in itself; for 'wisdom reacheth everywhere by reason of her purity.' It is in this absorption of wisdom that the Holy Ghost effects those glorious quiverings of His flame of which I am speaking. And as the flame is so sweet, the soul says: 'As Thou art no longer grievous.'

As Thou art no longer grievous,

19. Thou dost not afflict, nor vex, nor weary me as before. This flame, when the soul was in the state of spiritual purgation, that is, when it was entering that of contemplation, was not so friendly and sweet as it is now in the state of union. In order to explain this we must dwell a little on this point. For before the divine fire enters into the soul and unites itself to it in its inmost depth by the complete and perfect purgation and purity thereof, the flame, which is the Holy Ghost, wounds it, destroys and consumes the imperfections of its

evil habits. This is the work of the Holy Ghost, who thereby disposes the soul for its divine union and a substantial transformation in God by love. For the flame which afterwards unites itself to the soul, glorifying it, is the very same which before assailed and purified it; just as the fire which ultimately penetrates the substance of the fuel is the very same which in the beginning darted its flames around it, playing about it, and depriving it of its ugliness until it prepared it with its heat for its own entrance into it, and transformation of it into itself.

20. The soul suffers greatly in this spiritual exercise, and endures grievous afflictions of spirit which occasionally overflow into the senses; for then the flame is felt to be grievous, for in this state of purgation the flame does not burn brightly but is darksome, and if it gives forth any light at all it is only to show to the soul and make it feel all its miseries and defects; neither is it sweet but painful, and if it kindles a fire of love that fire causes torments and uneasiness; it does not bring delight but aridity, for although God in His kindness may send the soul some comfort to strengthen and animate it He makes it pay, both before and after, with sufferings and trials. It is not a refreshing and peaceful fire, but a consuming and searching one that makes the soul faint away and grieve at the sight of Self; not a glorious brightness, for it embitters the soul and makes it miserable, owing to the spiritual light it throws on Self, for, as Jeremias says, God 'hath sent fire into my bones' or, in the words of David 'Thou hast tried me by fire.' Thus, at this juncture, the soul suffers in the understanding from deep darkness, in the will from aridity and conflict, and in the memory from the consciousness of its miseries — for the eye of the spiritual understanding is clear — and in its very substance the soul suffers from poverty and dereliction. Dry and cold, yea, at times, even hot, nothing gives it relief, nor has it a single good thought to console it and to help it to lift up the heart to God, for this flame has made it 'grievous', even as Job said when he found himself in this plight: 'Thou art changed to be cruel toward me.' Suffering all these things together the soul undergoes, as it were, its Purgatory, for all happiness being taken away the torture is hardly inferior to the torments of Purgatory.

I should scarcely know how to describe this 'grievousness', and what the soul feels and bears in it were it not for these telling words of Jeremias: 'I am the man that see my poverty by the rod of His indignation; He hath led me, and brought me into darkness and not into light. Only against me He hath turned, and turned again His hand all the day. My skin and my flesh He hath made old, He hath broken my bones. He hath built round about me, and He hath encompassed me with gall and labour. He hath set me in dark places, as those that are dead for ever. He hath built against me round about, that I may not get out: He hath made my fetters heavy.' Jeremias says a great deal more besides this in the same place; for this is the remedy and medicine chosen by God to restore health to the soul after its many infirmities, the cure being of a necessity commensurate to the disease. Here, then, the heart is 'laid upon coals to drive away all kinds of devils'; here, too, all its maladies are brought to light, and openly exhibited before the eyes, and thus they are cured. Whatever may have been hidden within its depths now becomes visible and palpable to the soul by the glare and heat of that fire, for previously nothing could be seen. When the flame acts upon a log of wood steam and smoke are seen to issue in evidence of humidity and frigidity which were unsuspected beforehand. Thus the soul, near this flame, sees and feels clearly its miseries, because, O wonder! there arise within it contraries at variance with each other, yet seated side by side, making war against each other on the battlefield of the soul, and striving, as the philosophers say, to expel each other so as to reign uppermost in the soul. The virtues and properties of God, being in the highest degree perfect, arise and make war within the soul, on the habits and properties of man which are in the highest degree imperfect. For since this flame gives forth a dazzling light it penetrates the darkness of the soul which, in its way, is profound in the extreme; the soul now feels its natural darkness oppose the supernatural light, without feeling the supernatural light itself, for 'the darkness does not comprehend it.' Rather, it feels its natural darkness only in so far as it is penetrated by light, for no soul can see its own darkness except by the side of the Divine light until, the darkness being dissipated, itself becomes illumined and sees the light, the eye being now made clear and strong. For an intense light is to a weak sight, or an eye that is not wholly clear, nothing but darkness, because the excess of light destroys the power of seeing. For this reason the flame was 'grievous' to the eye of the understanding, for, being at once loving and tender, it lovingly and tenderly penetrates the will which, by its nature, is arid and hard. And as hardness is discovered when contrasted with tenderness, and aridity when compared with love, so the will comes to a knowledge of its own hardness and aridity when contrasted with God, though it does not feel the love and tenderness of the flame, for hardness and aridity cannot comprehend their contraries, until, being expelled by these, the love and tenderness of God reign supreme in the will, for two contraries cannot co-exist in one subject. Similarly, the soul perceives its own smallness in comparison with the immensity of the flame, and suffers great uneasiness until the flame, acting on it, dilates it. Thus, the latter has proved 'grievous' to the will also, for the sweet nourishment of love is insipid to a palate not yet weaned from other affections. Finally, the soul, which of itself is exceedingly poor, having nothing whatever, nor the means of procuring any satisfaction, gains a knowledge of its poverty, misery and malice by contrasting them with the riches, goodness and delights possessed by this flame, for malice does not comprehend goodness, nor poverty riches, etc., until the flame succeeds in purifying the soul, and, while transforming it, enriches, glorifies, and delights it too. In this manner the flame was at first 'grievous' to the soul, which suffers severely in its substance and powers from the uneasiness and anguish caused by the war of contraries within its ailing frame. Here, God Who is all perfection, there the habits of imperfection of the soul; cauterizing it with a Divine fire He extirpates them and leaves a well-prepared soil upon which He may enter with His gentle, peaceful and glorious love, as does a flame when it gets hold of wood.

So powerful a purgation is the lot of but few souls, namely of those whom He intends to lift by contemplation to some degree of union;

the more sublime that degree, the fiercer the purification. When He resolves to snatch a soul from the common way of natural operations and to lead it to the spiritual life, from meditation to contemplation – which is heavenly rather than earthly life – and to communicate Himself by the union of love, He begins by making Himself known to the spirit, as yet impure and imperfect and full of evil habits. Each one suffers in proportion to his imperfections. This purgation is sometimes as fierce in its way as that of Purgatory, for the one is meant to dispose the soul for a perfect union even here below, while the other is to enable it to see God hereafter. I shall say nothing here of the intention of this cleansing, the degrees of its intensity, its operation in the will, the understanding and the memory, in the substance of the soul, in all its powers, or in the sensitive part alone, nor how it may be ascertained whether it is this or that, at what time or at which precise point of the spiritual journey it begins, as all this has nothing to do with my present purpose; moreover, I have fully discussed it in my treatise on The Dark Night in *The Ascent of Mount Carmel*. It is enough for us to know that God, Who seeks to enter the soul by union and transformation of love, is He who previously assailed the soul, purifying it with the light and heat of His divine flame, just as it is the same fire that first disposes the wood for combustion and afterwards consumes it. Thus, the same which now is sweet, being seated within the soul, was at first 'grievous' while assailing it from without.

21. The meaning of the whole is as follows: Thou art now not only not darkness as before, but the divine light of my understanding wherewith I behold Thee: not only dost Thou abstain from causing me to faint in my weakness, but Thou art become the strength of my will, wherein I can love and enjoy Thee, being wholly transformed by divine love. Thou art no longer grief and affliction, but rather my glory, my delight, and my liberty, seeing that the words of the Canticle may be said of me, 'Who is this that cometh up from the desert flowing with delights leaning upon her Beloved,' scattering love on this side and on that? 'Perfect Thy work, if it be Thy Will.'

Perfect Thy work, if it be Thy Will,

22. That is, do Thou perfect the spiritual marriage in the beatific vision. Though it is true that the soul is the more resigned the more it is transformed, when it has attained to a state so high as this, for it knows nothing and seeks nothing with a view to itself, but only in and for the Beloved – for Charity seeks nothing but the good and glory of the Beloved – still because it lives in hope, and hope implies a want, it groans deeply – though sweetly and joyfully – because it has not fully attained to the perfect adoption of the sons of God, in which, being perfected in glory, all its desires will be satisfied. However intimate the soul's union may be with God, it will never be satisfied here below till His 'glory shall appear'; especially because it has already tasted, by anticipation, of its sweetness.

23. That sweetness is such that if God had not had pity on its natural frailty and covered it with His right hand, as He did Moses, that he might not die when he saw the glory of God – for the natural powers of the soul receive comfort and delight from that right hand, rather than hurt – it would have died at each vibration of the flame, seeing that the inferior part thereof is incapable of enduring so great and so sharp a fire. This desire of the soul is therefore no longer painful, for its condition is now such that all pain is over, and its prayers are offered for the object it desires in great sweetness, joy and resignation. This is the reason why it says, 'if it be Thy will,' for the will and desire are now so united in God, each in its own way, that the soul regards it as its glory that the will of God should be done in it. Such are now the glimpses of glory, and such the love which now shines forth, that it would argue but little love on its part if it did not pray to be admitted to the perfect consummation of love.

24. Moreover, the soul in the power of this sweet communication, sees that the Holy Ghost incites it, and invites it in most wonderful ways, and by sweet affections, to this immeasurable glory, which He there sets before it, saying, 'Arise, make haste, my love, my dove, my beautiful one, and come. For winter is now past, the rain is gone and departed. The flowers have appeared in our land . . .. The fig-tree hath brought forth her green figs, the flourishing vineyards have

given their savour. Arise, my love, my beautiful one, and come; my dove in the holes of the rock, in the hollow places of the wall, show me thy face, let thy voice sound in mine ears, for thy voice is sweet, and thy face comely.' The soul hears all this spoken by the Holy Ghost in this sweet and tender flame, and therefore answers Him, saying, 'Perfect Thy work, if it be Thy will,' thereby making the two petitions which our Lord commands, 'Thy kingdom come, Thy will be done'; that is, give me Thy kingdom according to Thy will, and that it may be so 'Break the web of this sweet encounter.'

Break the web of this sweet encounter.

25. That is, the hindrance to this so grand an affair. It is an easy thing to draw near unto God when all hindrances are set aside; and when the web that divides us from Him is broken. There are three webs to be broken before we can have the perfect fruition of God: 1. The temporal web, which comprises all created things. 2. The natural web, which comprises all mere natural actions and inclinations. 3. The web of sense, which is merely the union of soul and body; that is, the sensitive and animal life, of which St Paul speaks, saying, 'For we know if our earthly house of this habitation be dissolved, that we have a building of God, a house not made with hands, eternal in heaven.'

26. The first and second web must of necessity have been broken in order to enter into the fruition of God in the union of love, when we denied ourselves in worldly things and renounced them, when our affections and desires were mortified, and when all our operations became divine. These webs were broken in the assaults of this flame when it was still grievous. In the spiritual purgation the soul breaks the two webs I am speaking of, and becomes united with God; the third alone, the web of the life of sense remains now to be broken. This is the reason why but one web is mentioned here. For now one web alone remains, and this the flame assails not painfully and grievously as it assailed the others, but with great sweetness and delight.

27. Thus the death of such souls is most full of sweetness, beyond

that of their whole spiritual life, for they die of the sweet violence of love, like the swan which sings more sweetly when death is nigh.

28. This is why the Psalmist said, 'Precious in the sight of our Lord is the death of His saints,' for then the rivers of the soul's love flow into the sea of love, so wide and deep as to seem a sea themselves; the beginning and the end unite together to accompany the just departing for His kingdom. 'From the ends of the earth', in the words of Isaias, are 'heard praises, the glory of the just one,' and the soul feels itself in the midst of these glorious encounters on the point of departing in all abundance for the perfect fruition of the kingdom, for it beholds itself pure and rich, and prepared, so far as it is possible, consistently with the faith and the conditions of this life. God now permits it to behold its own beauty, and intrusts it with the gifts and graces He has endowed it with, for all this turns into love and praise without the stain of presumption or of vanity, because no leaven of imperfection remains to corrupt it.

29. When the soul sees that nothing is wanting but the breaking of the frail web of its natural life, by which its liberty is enthralled, it prays that it may be broken; for it longs 'to be dissolved and to be with Christ,' to burst the bonds which bind the spirit and the flesh together, that both may resume their proper state, for they are by nature different, the flesh to 'return to its earth, and the spirit unto God Who gave it.' The mortal body, as St John saith, 'profiteth nothing', but is rather a hindrance to the good of the spirit. The soul, therefore, prays for the dissolution of the body, for it is sad that a life so mean should be a hindrance in the way of a life so noble.

30. This life is called a web for three reasons: 1. Because of the connection between the spirit and the flesh. 2. Because it separates the soul and God. 3. Because a web is not so thick but that light penetrates it. The connection between soul and body, in this state of perfection, is so slight a web that the divinity shines through it, now that the soul is so spiritualized, subtilized, and refined. When the power of the life to come is felt in the soul, the weakness of this life becomes manifest. Its present life seems to be but a slender web, even a spider's web, in the words of David, 'our years shall be

considered as a spider,' and even less than that, when the soul is raised to a state so high, for being raised so high, it perceives things as God does, in Whose sight 'a thousand years are as yesterday which is past,' and before Whom 'all nations are as if they had no being at all.' In the same way all things appear to the soul as nothing, yea, itself is nothing in its own eyes, and God alone is its all.

31. It may be asked here why the soul prays for the breaking of the web rather than for its cutting or its removal, since the effect would be the same in either case. There are four reasons which determine it: 1. The expression it employs is the most proper, because it is more natural that a thing should be broken in an encounter, than that it should be cut or taken away. 2. Because love likes force, with violent and impetuous contacts, and these result in breaking rather than in cutting or taking away. 3. Because its love is so strong, it desires that the act of breaking the web may be done in a moment; the more rapid and spiritual the act, the greater its force and worth.

32. The power of love is now more concentrated and more vigorous, and the perfection of transforming love enters the soul, as form into matter, in an instant. Until now there was no act of perfect transformation, only the disposition towards it in desires and affections successively repeated, which in very few souls attain to the perfect act of transformation. Hence a soul that is disposed may elicit many more, and more intense acts in a brief period than another soul not so disposed in a long time, for this soul spends all its energies in the preparation of itself, and even afterwards the fire does not wholly penetrate the fuel it has to burn. But when the soul is already prepared, love enters in continuously, and the spark at the first contact seizes on the fuel that is dry. And thus the enamoured soul prefers the abrupt breaking of the web to its tedious cutting or waiting for its removal.

33. 4. The fourth reason why the soul prays for the breaking of the web of life is its desire that it may be done quickly: for when we cut or remove anything we do it deliberately, when the matter is ripe, and then time and thought become necessary; but a violent rupture requires nothing of the kind. The soul's desire is not to wait for the

natural termination of its mortal life, because the violence of its love and the disposition it is in incline it with resignation towards the violent rupture of its natural life in the supernatural assaults of love. Moreover, it knows well that it is the way of God to call such souls to Himself before the time, that He fills them with good, and delivers them from evil, perfecting them in a short space, and bestowing upon them, through love, what they could have gained only by length of time. 'Pleasing God, he is made beloved, and living among sinners he was translated. He was taken away lest malice should change his understanding, or lest any guile deceive his soul. Being consummate in a short space, he fulfilled much time, for his soul pleased God; for this cause He hastened to bring him out of the midst of iniquities.' The constant practice of love is therefore a matter of the last importance, for when the soul is perfect therein, its detention here below cannot be long before it is admitted to see God face to face.

34. But why is this interior assault of the Holy Ghost called an encounter? Though the soul is very desirous to see the end of its natural life, yet because the time is not yet come, that cannot be, and so God, to make it perfect and to raise it above the flesh more and more, assails it divinely and gloriously, and these assaults are really encounters wherein God penetrates the soul, deifies the very substance of it, and renders it as it were divine. The substance of God absorbs the soul, because He assails and pierces it to the quick by the Holy Ghost, whose communications are vehement when they are of fire as at present. The soul says this encounter is sweet, because it has therein a lively taste of God; not that many other touches and encounters of God, of which the soul is now the object, cease to be sweet and delicious, but on account of the supereminent sweetness of this; for God effects it in order to detach it perfectly and make it glorious. Hence the soul relying on His protection becomes bold, and says, 'Break the web of this sweet encounter.'

35. The whole stanza may be paraphrased as follows: O flame of the Holy Ghost, penetrating so profoundly and so tenderly the very substance of my soul, and burning it with Thy heat, since Thou art

now so gentle as to manifest Thy desire of giving Thyself wholly to me in everlasting life; if formerly my petitions did not reach Thine ears, when I was weary and worn with love, suffering through the weakness of sense and spirit, because of my great infirmities, impurity, and little love, I prayed to be set free – for with desire hath my soul desired Thee – when my impatient love would not suffer me to submit to the conditions of this life according to Thy will – for it was Thy will that I should live – and when the previous impulses of my love were insufficient in Thy sight, because there was no substance in them; now that I am grown strong in love, that body and soul together do not only follow after Thee, but that my heart and my flesh rejoice in the living God with one consent, so that I am praying for that which Thou willest I should pray for, and what Thou willest not, that I pray not for – it seems even that I could not do it, neither does it enter into my mind to do so – and as my prayers are now more efficacious and more reasonable in Thy sight, for they proceed from Thee, and Thou willest I should so pray, and as I pray in the joy and sweetness of the Holy Ghost, and 'my judgment cometh forth from Thy countenance,' when Thou art pleased with my prayer and hearkenest to it – break Thou the slender web of this life that I may be enabled to love Thee hereafter with that fullness and abundance which my soul desires, without end for evermore.

STANZA II

O sweet burn!
O delicious wound!
O tender hand! O gentle touch !
Savouring of everlasting life,
And paying the whole debt,
In destroying death Thou hast changed it into life.

EXPLANATION

We learn here that it is the Three Persons of the Most Holy Trinity, Father, Son, and Holy Ghost, Who accomplish the divine work of union in the soul. The 'hand', the 'touch', and the 'burn' are in substance one and the same; and the three terms are employed because they express effects peculiar to each. The 'burn' is the Holy Ghost; the 'hand' is the Father; and the 'touch' is the Son. Thus the soul magnifies the Father, the Son, and the Holy Ghost, extolling those three grand gifts and graces which They perfect within it, in that They have changed death into life, transforming it in Themselves.

2. The first of these gifts is the delicious wound, attributed to the Holy Ghost, and so the soul calls it the 'burn'. The second is the 'taste of everlasting life', attributed to the Son, and the soul calls it the 'gentle touch'. The third is that 'gift' which is the perfect recompense of the soul, attributed to the Father, and is therefore called the 'tender hand.' Though the Three Persons of the Most Holy Trinity are referred to severally, because of the operations peculiar to Each, the soul is addressing itself to but One Essence, saying, 'Thou hast changed it into life,' for the Three Divine Persons work together, and the whole is attributed to Each, and to All.

O sweet burn!

3. In the book of Deuteronomium, Moses saith, 'Our Lord God is a consuming fire,' that is, a fire of love. And as His power is infinite, He consumes infinitely, burning with great vehemence, and transforming into Himself all He touches. But He burns everything according to the measure of its preparation, some more, others less; and also according to His own good pleasure, as, and when, and how, He will. And as this is an infinite fire of love, so when He touches the soul somewhat sharply, the burning heat within it becomes so extreme as to surpass all the fires of the world. This is the reason why this touch of God is said to be a 'burn': for the fire there is more intense, and more concentrated, and the effect of it surpasses that of all other fires.

4. When the divine fire shall have transformed the soul into itself, the soul not only feels the burn, but itself is become wholly and entirely burnt up in this vehement fire. O how wonderful the fire of God! though so vehement and so consuming, though it can destroy a thousand worlds with more ease than the material fire can destroy a single straw, it consumes not the spirit wherein it burns, but rather, in proportion to its strength and heat, delights and deifies it, burning sweetly within according to the strength which God has given. Thus, on the day of Pentecost the fire descended with great vehemence upon the Apostles, who, according to St Gregory, sweetly burned interiorly. The Church also says, when celebrating that event: 'The divine fire came down, not consuming but enlightening.' For as the object of these communications is to elevate the soul, the burning of the fire does not distress it but gladdens it, does not weary it but delights it, and renders it glorious and rich. This is the reason why it is said to be sweet.

5. Thus then the blessed soul, which by the mercy of God has been burnt, knoweth all things, tasteth all things, 'whatsoever it shall do shall prosper,' against it nothing shall prevail, nothing shall touch it. It is of that soul that the Apostle said: 'The spiritual man judgeth all things, and he himself is judged of no man,' for 'the Spirit searcheth all things, yea, the deep things of God,' because it belongs to love to search into all that the Beloved has.

6. O, the great glory of the souls who are worthy of this supreme fire which, having infinite power to consume and annihilate you, consumes you not, but makes you infinitely perfect in glory! Wonder not that God should elevate some souls to so high a degree, for He alone is wonderful in His marvellous works. As this burn then is so sweet – as it is here said to be – how happy must that soul be which this fire has touched! The soul would speak of it, but cannot, so it says only, 'O delicious wound.'

O delicious wound!

7. He Who inflicts the wound relieves, and heals while He inflicts it. It bears some resemblance to the caustic usage of natural fire,

which when applied to a wound increases it, and renders a wound, which iron or other instruments occasioned, a wound of fire. The longer the caustic is applied, the more grievous the wound, until the whole matter be destroyed. Thus the divine burn of love heals the wound which love has caused, and by each application renders it greater. The healing which love brings is to wound again what was wounded before, until the soul melts away in the fire of love. So when the soul shall become wholly one wound of love it will then be transformed in love, wounded with love. For herein he who is most wounded is the most healthy, and he who is all wound is all health.

8. And yet even if the whole soul be one wound, and consequently sound, the divine burning is not intermitted; it continues its work, which is to wound the soul with love. But then, too, its work is to soothe the healed wound, and the soul therefore cries out, 'O delicious wound,' and so much the more delicious the more penetrating the fire of love. The Holy Ghost inflicted the wound that He might soothe it, and as His will and desire to soothe it are great, great will be the wound which He will inflict, in order that the soul He has wounded may be greatly comforted. O blessed wound inflicted by Him Who cannot but heal it!

9. O happy and most blessed wound! For thou art inflicted only for the joy and comfort of the soul. Great is the wound, because He is great Who has wrought it; and great is the delight of it: for the fire of love is infinite. O delicious wound then, and the more delicious the more the burn of love penetrates the inmost substance of the soul, burning all it can burn that it may supply all the delight it can give. This burning and wound, in my opinion, are the highest condition attainable in this life. There are many other forms of this burning, but they do not reach so far, neither are they like unto this: for this is the touch of the Divinity without form or figure, either natural, formal, or imaginary.

10. But the soul is burned in another and most excellent way, which is this: when a soul is on fire with love, but not in the degree of which I am now speaking – though it should be so, that it may be the subject of this – it will feel as if a seraph with a burning brand of love

had struck it, and penetrated it already on fire as glowing coal, or rather as a flame, and burns it utterly. And then in that burn the flame rushes forth and surges vehemently as in a glowing furnace or forge; the fire revives and the flame ascends when the burning fuel is disturbed. Then when the burning brand touches it, the soul feels that the wound it has thus received is delicious beyond all imagination. For beside being altogether moved or stirred, at the time of this stirring of the fire, by the vehement movement of the seraph, wherein the ardour and the melting of love is great, it feels that its wound is perfect, and that the herbs which serve to attemper the steel are efficacious; it feels the very depths of the spirit transpierced, and its delight to be exquisite beyond the power of language to express. The soul feels, as it were, a most minute grain of mustard seed, most pungent and burning in the inmost heart of the spirit; in the spot of the wound, where the substance and the power of the herb reside, diffuse itself most subtilely through all the spiritual veins of the soul in proportion to the strength and power of the heat. It feels its love to grow, strengthen, and refine itself to such a degree, as to seem to itself as if seas of fire were in it filling it with love.

11. The fruition of the soul now cannot be described otherwise than by saying that it understands why the kingdom of heaven is compared in the Gospel to a mustard seed, which by reason of its great natural heat grows into a lofty tree. 'The kingdom of heaven is like a grain of mustard seed, which a man took and sowed in his field. Which is the least surely of all seeds; but when it is grown up, it is greater than all herbs, and is made a tree, so that the fowls of the air come and dwell in the branches thereof.' The soul beholds itself now as one immense sea of fire. Few souls, however, attain to this state, but some have done so, especially those whose spirit and power is to be transmitted to their spiritual children; since God bestows on the founder gifts and graces, according to the succession of the order in the first-fruits of the Spirit.

12. To return to the work of the seraph, which in truth is to strike and wound. If the effect of the wound be permitted to flow exteriorly into the bodily senses, an effect corresponding to the interior wound

itself will manifest itself without. Thus it was with St Francis, for when the seraph wounded his soul with love, the effects of that wound became outwardly visible. God confers no favours on the body which He does not confer in the first place chiefly on the soul. In that case, the greater the joy and violence of the love which is the cause of the interior wound, the greater will be the pain of the visible wound, and as the former grows so does the latter.

13. The reason is this: such souls as these, being already purified and strong in God, their spirit, strong and sound, delights in the strong and sweet Spirit of God; Who, however, causes pain and suffering in their weak and corruptible flesh. It is thus a most marvellous thing to feel pain and sweetness together. Job felt it when he said, 'Returning, Thou tormentest me wonderfully.' This is marvellous, worthy of the multitude of the sweetness of God, which He has hidden for them that fear Him; the greater the sweetness and delight, the greater the pain and suffering.

14. O Infinite greatness, in all things showing Thyself omnipotent. Who, O Lord, can cause sweetness in the midst of bitterness, and pleasure in the midst of pain? O delicious wound, the greater the delight the deeper the wound. But when the wound is within the soul, and not communicated to the body without, it is then much more intense and keen. As the flesh is bridle to the spirit, so, when the graces of the latter overflow into the former, the flesh draws in and restrains the swift steed of the spirit and checks its course; 'for the corruptible body is a load upon the soul, and the earthly habitation presseth down the mind that museth upon many things.' He, therefore, who shall trust much to the bodily senses will never become a very spiritual man.

15. This I say for the sake of those who think they can ascend to the heights and power of the spirit, by the mere energy and action of the senses, which are mean and vile. We cannot become spiritual unless the bodily sense be restrained. It is a state of things wholly different from this, when the spirit overflows into the senses, for there may be great spirituality in this; as in the case of St Paul, whose deep sense of the sufferings of Christ overflowed into his body, so

that he said: 'I bear the marks of our Lord Jesus in my body.' Thus, as the wound and the burn, so the hand that inflicted it; and as the touch, so He who touched. 'O tender hand, O gentle touch.'

O tender hand! O gentle touch!

16. O hand, as generous as Thou art powerful and rich, giving me gifts with power. O gentle hand! laid so gently upon me, and yet, if Thou wert to press at all, the whole world must perish; for only at the sight of Thee the earth trembles, the nations melt, and the mountains are crushed in pieces. O gentle hand, I say it again, for him thou didst touch so sharply. Upon me Thou art laid so softly, so lovingly, and so tenderly; Thou art the more gentle and sweet for me than thou wert hard for him; the loving sweetness with which Thou art laid upon me is greater than the severity with which he was touched. Thou killest, and Thou givest life, and there is no one who shall escape out of Thy hand.

17. But Thou, O divine life, never killest but to give life, as Thou never woundest but to heal. Thou hast wounded me, O divine hand! that Thou mayest heal me. Thou hast slain in me that which made me dead, and without the life of God which I now live. This Thou hast wrought in the liberality of Thy gracious generosity, through that touch, wherewith Thou dost touch me, of the brightness of Thy glory and the figure of Thy substance, Thine only begotten Son, in Whom being Thy Wisdom, Thou reachest 'from end to end mightily.'

18. O gentle, subtile touch, the Word, the Son of God, Who, because of the pureness of Thy divine nature, dost penetrate subtilely the very substance of my soul, and, touching it gently, absorbest it wholly in divine ways of sweetness not 'heard of in the land of Canaan', nor 'seen in Teman'. O touch of the Word, so gentle, so wonderfully gentle to me; and yet Thou wert 'over-throwing mountains, and breaking rocks in Horeb', by the shadow of Thy power going before, when Thou didst announce Thy presence to the prophet in 'the whisper of a gentle air'. O soft air, how is it that Thou touchest so softly when Thou art so terrible and so strong? O

blessed soul, most blessed, which Thou, who art so terrible and so strong, touchest so gently. Proclaim it to the world, O my soul – no, proclaim it not, for the world knoweth not the 'gentle air', neither will it listen to it, because it cannot comprehend matters so deep.

19. O my God and my life, they shall know Thee and behold Thee when Thou touchest them, who, making themselves strangers upon earth, shall purify themselves, because purity corresponds with purity. The more gently Thou touchest, the more Thou art hidden in the purified soul of those who have made themselves strangers here, hidden from the face of all creatures, and whom 'Thou shalt hide in the secret of Thy face from the disturbance of men.'

20. O, again and again, gentle touch, which by the power of its tenderness, undoest the soul, removest it far away from every touch whatever, and makest it Thine own; Thou which leavest behind Thee effects and impressions so pure, that the touch of everything else seems vile and low, the very sight offensive, and all relations therewith a deep affliction. The more subtile any matter is, the more it spreads and fills, and the more it diffuses itself the more subtile is it. O gentle touch, the more subtile the more infused. And now the vessel of my soul, because Thou hast touched it, is pure and clean and able to receive Thee.

21. O gentle touch! as in Thee there is nothing material, so Thy touch is the more penetrating, changing what in me is human into divine, for Thy Divine essence, wherewith Thou touchest me, is wholly unaffected by modes and manner, free from the husks of form and figure. Finally then, O gentle touch, and most gentle, for Thou touchest me with Thy most simple and pure essence, which being infinite is infinitely gentle; therefore it is that this touch is so subtile, so loving, so deep, and so delicious.

Savouring of everlasting life,

22. What the soul tastes now in this touch of God, is, in truth, though not perfectly, a certain foretaste of everlasting life, as I said before. It is not incredible that it should be so when we believe, as we

do believe, that this touch is most substantial, and that the substance of God touches the substance of the soul. Many saints have experienced it in this life. The sweetness of delight which this touch occasions baffles all description. Neither will I speak of it, lest men should suppose that it is nothing beyond what my words imply, for there are no terms by which we can designate or explain the deep things of God transacted in perfect souls. The proper way to speak of them is for him who has been favoured with them to understand them, feel them, and enjoy them, and be silent.

23. For the soul now sees that they are in some measure like the white counter of which it is written 'To him that overcometh I will give . . . a white counter, and in the counter a new name written, which no man knoweth but he that receiveth it.' Thus it may be truly said, 'savouring of everlasting life'. For though the fruition of it is not perfect in this life as it will be in glory; nevertheless the touch, being of God, savoureth of everlasting life, and accordingly the soul tastes in a marvellous manner, and by participation, of all the things of God; fortitude, wisdom, love, beauty, grace, and goodness being communicated unto it.

24. Now as God is all this, the soul tastes of all in one single touch of God in a certain eminent way. And from this good bestowed upon the soul, some of the unction of the Spirit overflows at times into the body itself, penetrating into the very bones, as it is written, 'All my bones shall say: Lord, who is like unto Thee?' But as all I can say falls short of the subject, it is enough to repeat, 'savouring of everlasting life'.

And paying the whole debt,

25. But what debts are they to which the soul here refers, and which it declares to be paid or satisfied? We should know that souls which attain to this high state, to the kingdom of the spiritual betrothal, have in general passed through many tribulations and trials, because it is 'through many tribulations that we enter into the kingdom of heaven'. And these tribulations are now passed.

26. What they have to suffer who are to attain unto union with

God, are divers afflictions and temptations of sense, trials, tribulations, temptations, darkness, and distress of mind, so that both the flesh and the spirit may be purified together, as I said in *The Dark Night* in my treatise of *The Ascent of Mount Carmel*. The reason is that the joy and knowledge of God cannot be established in the soul, if the flesh and spirit are not perfectly purified and spiritualized, and as trials and penances purify and refine the senses, as tribulations, temptations, darkness and distress spiritualize and prepare the spirit, so they must undergo them who would be transformed in God – as the souls in purgatory who through that trial attain to the beatific vision – some more intensely than others, some for a longer, others for a shorter time, according to those degrees of union to which God intends to raise them, and according to their need of purification.

27. It is by these trials to which God subjects the spirit and the flesh that the soul, in bitterness, acquires virtues and fortitude and perfection, as the Apostle writes, 'Power is made perfect in infirmity'; for virtue is made perfect in weakness, and refined by sufferings. Iron cannot be fashioned according to the pattern of the artificer but by fire and the hammer, and during the process its previous condition is injured. This is the way in which God taught Jeremias, 'From on high He hath cast a fire in my bones and hath taught me.' The prophet speaks of the hammer also when he saith, 'Thou hast chastised me, and I am taught.' So, too, the Wise Man asks, 'He that hath not been proved, what knoweth he?'

28. Here comes the question, why is it that so few ever attain to this state? The reason is that, in this marvellous work which God Himself begins, so many are weak, shrinking from trouble, and unwilling to endure the least discomfort or mortification, or to labour with constant patience. Hence it is that God, not finding them diligent in cultivating the graces He has given them when He began to try them, proceeds no further with their purification, neither does He lift them up out of the dust of the earth, because it required greater courage and resolution for this than they possessed.

29. Thus it may be said to those who desire to advance, but who

will not endure a lighter trial nor submit themselves thereto, in the words of Jeremias, 'If with running with footmen thou hast laboured how canst thou contend with horses? and whereas in a land of peace thou hast been secure, what wilt thou do in the pride of Jordan?' That is, if the ordinary trials of human life to which all men living are liable are wearisome and a burden for thee, how art thou to 'contend with horses'? that is, how canst thou venture out of the common trials of life upon others of greater violence and swiftness? If thou hast been unwilling to make war against the peace and pleasures of the earth, thine own sensuality, but rather seekest comfort and tranquillity on it, what wilt thou do in the pride of Jordan? that is, how wilt thou stand against the rushing waters of tribulations and the more interior trials of the spirit?

30. O souls that seek your own ease and comfort, if you knew how necessary for this high state is suffering, and how profitable suffering and mortification are for attaining to these great blessings, you would never seek for comfort anywhere, but you would rather take up the cross with the vinegar and the gall, and would count it an inestimable favour, knowing that by thus dying to the world and to your own selves, you would live to God in spiritual joy; in the patient endurance of your exterior afflictions you would merit at the hands of God, that He should look upon you, cleanse and purify you more and more in these spiritual tribulations. They whom He thus blesses must have served Him well and long, must have been patient and persevering, and their life most pleasing in His sight. The angel said unto Tobias 'Because thou wast acceptable to God, it was necessary that temptation should prove thee.' Tobias was acceptable to God, therefore He tried him; He gave him the grace of tribulation, the source of greater graces still, and it is written of him that 'the rest of his life was in joy'.

31. The same truth is exemplified in the life of Job. God acknowledged him as His faithful servant in the presence of the angels good and evil, and immediately sent him heavy trials, that He might afterwards raise him higher, as He did, both in temporal and spiritual things.

32. This is the way God deals with those whom it is His will to

exalt. He suffers them to be tempted, afflicted, tormented and chastened, inwardly and outwardly, to the utmost limit of their strength, that He may deify them, unite them to Himself in His wisdom, which is the highest state, purifying them, first in that wisdom, as David observed, saying that the 'words of our Lord are chaste words, silver, examined by fire,' tested in the earth of our flesh and purified seven times, that is, made perfectly pure.

33. It is not necessary I should stop here to say how each of these purgations tends to the divine wisdom, which in this life is as silver, for however pure it may be, yet is not comparable to the pure gold, which is reserved for everlasting glory.

34. But it is very necessary for the soul to endure these tribulations and trials, inward and outward, spiritual and corporal, great and small, with great resolution and patience, accepting all as from the hand of God for its healing and its good, not shrinking from them, because they are for the health of the soul. 'If the spirit of him that hath power', saith the Wise Man, 'ascend upon thee, leave not thy place, because carefulness' – that is healing – 'will make the greatest sins to cease.' 'Leave not thy place', that is, the place of thy trial, which is thy troubles; for the healing which they bring will break the thread of thy sins and imperfections, which is evil habits, so that they shall proceed no further. Thus, interior trials and tribulations destroy and purge away the imperfect and evil habits of the soul. We are, therefore, to count it a great favour when our Lord sends us interior and exterior trials, remembering that they are few in number who deserve to be made perfect through sufferings so as to attain to so high a state as this.

35. I return to the explanation of the words before me. The soul now remembers that its past afflictions are most abundantly recompensed, for 'as the darkness so also the light thereof', and that having once been 'a partaker of the sufferings', it is now 'of the consolation', that its interior and exterior trials have been recompensed by the divine mercies, none of them being without its corresponding reward. It therefore acknowledges itself perfectly satisfied, and says, 'paying the whole debt,' as David did, 'How great tribula-

tions hast Thou shown me, many and evil, and turning Thou hast quickened me, and from the depths of the earth Thou hast brought me back again. Thou hast multiplied Thy magnificence, and turning to me Thou hast comforted me.'

36. Thus the soul which once stood without at the gates of the palace of God – like Mardochai weeping in the streets of Susan because his life was threatened, clothed with sackcloth and refusing the garments which Esther sent him, unrewarded for his faithful service in defending the king's honour and life, – finds, also, like Mardochai, all its trials and service rewarded in one day. It is not only admitted within the palace and stands in royal robes before the king, but has also a diadem on its head, and in its hand a sceptre, and sitting on the royal throne with the king's signet on its finger, symbols of its power in the kingdom of the Bridegroom. For those souls who attain to this high state obtain all their desires; the whole debt is amply paid: the appetites, their enemies which sought their life, are dead, while they are living in God. 'In destroying death Thou hast changed it into life.'

Thou hast changed death into life.

37. Death is nothing else but the privation of life, for when life cometh there is no trace of death in that which is spiritual. There are two kinds of life, one beatific, consisting in the vision of God, and this must be preceded by a natural and bodily death, as it is written, 'We know if our earthly house of this habitation be dissolved, that we have a building of God, a house not made with hands, eternal in heaven.' The other is the perfect spiritual life, consisting in the possession of God by the union of love. Men attain to this through the mortification of their evil habits and desires. Until this be done, the perfection of the spiritual life of union with God is unattainable, 'For', as the Apostle saith, 'if you live according to the flesh, you shall die: but if by the spirit you mortify the deeds of the flesh, you shall live.'

38. By 'death' here is meant the old man, that is the employment of our faculties, memory, understanding, and will, upon the things

of this world, and the desire on the pleasure which created things supply. All this is the old life; it is the death of the new life which is spiritual, and which the soul cannot live perfectly unless to the old man it be perfectly dead, for so the Apostle teaches, when he bids us put 'away according to the old conversation, the old man ... and put on the new man, which, according to God, is created in justice and holiness of the truth.' In this new life, when the soul shall have attained to perfect union with God, all its affections, powers, and acts, in themselves imperfect and vile, become as it were divine. And as everything that lives, to use the expression of philosophers, lives in its acts, so the soul, having its acts in God by virtue of its union with Him, lives the life of God, its death being changed into life.

39. This is so, because the understanding, which, previous to its union with God, understood but dimly by means of its natural light, is now under the influence and direction of another principle, and of a higher illumination of God. The will, which previously loved but weakly, is now changed into the life of divine love, for now it loves deeply with the affections of divine love, moved by the Holy Ghost in whom it now lives. The memory, which once saw nothing but the forms and figures of created things, is now changed, and keeps in 'mind the eternal years', as David spoke. The desire, which previously longed for created food, now tastes and relishes the food that is divine, influenced by another and more efficacious principle, the sweetness of God.

40. Finally, all the motions and acts of the soul, proceeding from the principle of its natural and imperfect life, are now changed in this union with God into motions divine. For the soul, as the true child of God, is moved by the Spirit of God, as it is written, 'Whosoever are led by the Spirit of God, they are the sons of God.' The substance of the soul, though it is not the substance of God, because inconvertible into Him, yet being united to Him and absorbed in Him, is by participation God. This is accomplished in the perfect state of the spiritual life, but not so perfectly as in the other; hence is it well said: 'While slaying thou hast changed death into life.'

41. The soul, therefore, has good reason for saying with St Paul,

'I live, now not I, but Christ liveth in me.' What in the soul is dead and cold, becomes changed into the life of God, the soul 'swallowed up of life' in fulfilling the words of the Apostle, 'Death is swallowed up in victory,' and those of Osee, 'I will be thy death, O death.'

42. The soul being thus swallowed up of life, detached from all secular and temporal things, and delivered from the disorderliness of nature, is led into the chamber of the King, where it rejoices and is glad in the Beloved, remembering His breasts more than wine, and saying, 'I am black but beautiful, O ye daughters of Jerusalem,' for my natural blackness is changed into the beauty of the heavenly King. O then, the burning of the fire! infinitely burning above all other fires, O how infinitely beyond all other fires dost thou burn me, and the more thou burnest the sweeter thou art to me. 'O delicious wound,' more delicious to me than all the delights and health of the world. 'O tender hand,' infinitely more tender than all tenderness, and the greater the pressure of it the more tender is it to me. 'O gentle touch,' the gentleness of which surpasses infinitely all the gentleness and all the loveliness of created things, sweeter and more delicious than honey and the honeycomb, because thou savourest of everlasting life; and is the more sweet the more profoundly thou dost touch me. Thou art infinitely more precious than gold and precious stones, for thou payest debts which nothing else can pay, because thou changest marvellously death into life.

43. In this state of life, so perfect, the soul is, as it were, keeping a perpetual feast with the praises of God in its mouth, with a new song of joy and love, full of the knowledge of its high dignity. It sometimes exulteth, repeating the words of Job, 'My glory shall always be renewed', and 'as a palm tree' I 'will multiply days.' That is, God will not suffer my glory to grow old as before, and He will multiply my days, that is, my merits, unto heaven, as a palm tree multiplies its branches. And also the words of David in the twenty-ninth Psalm, the soul sings interiorly to God, especially the conclusion thereof, 'Thou hast turned my mourning into joy unto me: Thou hast cut my sackcloth and hast compassed me with gladness, that my glory may sing to Thee, and I be not compunct' – for this state is inaccessible to

pain – 'Lord my God, for ever will I confess to Thee.'

44. Here the soul is so conscious of God's solicitude to comfort it, feeling that He is Himself encouraging it with words so precious, so tender, so endearing; that He is conferring graces upon it, one upon another, so that it seems as if there were no other soul in the world for Him to comfort, no other object of His care, but that everything was done for this one soul alone. This truth is admitted by the bride in the Canticle when she says, 'My Beloved to me and I to Him.'

STANZA III

O lamps of fire,
In the splendours of which
The deep caverns of sense,
Dim and dark,
With unwonted brightness
Give light and warmth together to their Beloved.

EXPLANATION

I stand greatly in need of the help of God to enter into the deep meaning of this stanza: great attention also is necessary on the part of the reader, for if he be without experience of the matter he will find it very obscure, while, on the other hand, it will be clear and full of sweetness to him who has had that experience.

2. In this stanza the soul most heartily thanks the Bridegroom for the great mercies which, in the state of union, it has received at His hands, for He has given therein a manifold and most profound knowledge of Himself, which enlightens its powers and senses, and fills them with love. These powers, previous to the state of union, were in darkness and blindness, but are now illumined by the fires of

love and respond thereto, offering that very light and love to Him who has kindled and inspired them by infusing into the soul gifts so divine. For he who truly loves is satisfied then when his whole self, all he is, all he can be, all he has, and all he can acquire, is spent in the service of his love; and the greater that service the greater is his pleasure in giving it. Such is the joy of the soul now, because it can shine in the presence of the Beloved in the splendours with which He has surrounded it, and love Him with that love which He has communicated to it.

O lamps of fire,

3. Lamps have two properties, that of giving light and of burning. If we are to understand this stanza, we must keep in mind, that God in His one and simple essence is all the power and majesty of His attributes. He is omnipotent, wise, good, merciful, just, strong, loving; He is all the other attributes and perfections of which we have no knowledge here below. He is all this. When the soul is in union with Him, and He is pleased to admit it to a special knowledge of Himself, the soul sees in Him all these perfections and majesty together in the one and simple essence clearly and distinctly, so far as it is consistent with the faith, and as each one of these attributes is the very being of God, Who is the Father, the Son, and the Holy Ghost – as each attribute is God Himself – and as God is infinite light, and infinite divine fire, it follows that each attribute gives light and burns as God Himself. God therefore, according to this knowledge of Him in unity, is to the soul as many lamps, because it has the knowledge of each of them, and because they minister to it the warmth of love, each in its own way, and yet all of one substance, all one lamp. This lamp is all lamps, because it gives light, and burns, in all ways.

4. The soul seeing this, the one lamp is to it as many lamps, for though but one, it can do all things, and has all power and comprehends every spirit. And thus it may be said that the one lamp shines and burns many ways in one: it shines and burns as omnipotent, as wise, as good, ministering to the soul knowledge and love, and

revealing itself unto it, according to the measure of its strength for the reception of all. The splendour of the lamp as omnipotent gives to the soul the light and warmth of the love of God as omnipotent, and accordingly God is now the lamp of omnipotence to the soul, shining and burning according to that attribute. The splendour of the lamp as wisdom produces the warmth of the love of God as all wise, and so of the other attributes; for the light which emanates from each of the attributes of God and from all the others, produces in the soul the fire of the love of God as such. Thus God is to the soul in these communications and manifestations of Himself – they are, I think, the highest possible in this life – as innumerable lamps from which light and love proceed.

5. These lamps revealed Him to Moses on Mount Sinai, where God passed before Him, and where Moses fell prostrate on the earth in all haste. He mentions some of the perfections of God which he then saw, and, loving Him in them, speaks of them separately in the following words: 'O Lord God, merciful and clement, patient and of much compassion, and true, who keepest mercy unto thousands; Who takest away iniquity and wicked deeds and sin, and no man of himself is innocent before Thee.' It appears that the principal attributes of God which Moses then recognized and loved were those of omnipotence, dominion, mercy, justice and truth which was a most profound knowledge, and the deepest delight of love.

6. It follows from this that the joy and rapture of love communicated to the soul in the fire of the light of these lamps is admirable, and immeasurable: as abundant as from many lamps, each of which burns with love, the heat of one subserving that of the other, as the light of one ministers to that of the other; all of them forming but one light and fire, and each of them that one fire. The soul, too, infinitely absorbed in these delicious flames, is subtilely wounded by each one of them, and by all of them more subtilely and more profoundly, in the love of life; the soul sees clearly that this love is everlasting life, which is the union of all blessings, and recognizes the truth of those words, 'The lamps thereof lamps of fire and flames.'

7. If 'a great and darksome horror seized upon' Abram as he saw

one 'lamp of fire passing' before him, when he learned with what rigorous justice God was about to visit the Chananeans, shall not the lamps of the knowledge of God shining now sweetly and lovingly produce greater light and joy of love than that one lamp produced of horror and darkness, when it passed before Abram? O my soul! how great, how excellent, and how manifold, will be thy light and joy: seeing that in all, and by all, thou shalt feel that He gives thee His own joy and love, loving thee according to His powers, attributes, and properties. For he who loves and does good to another honours him and does him good according to his own nature and qualities. Thus the Bridegroom abiding in thee, being all-powerful, gives Himself to thee, and loves thee with all power; being wise, with wisdom; being good, with goodness; being holy, with holiness. And as He is liberal thou wilt feel also that He loves thee with liberality, without self-interest, only to do thee good, showing joyfully His countenance full of grace, and saying: I am thine and for thee, and it is My pleasure to be what I am, that I may give Myself to thee and be thine.

8. Who then shall describe thy feeling, O blessed soul, when thus beloved, and so highly honoured? 'Thy belly as a heap of wheat compassed about with lilies.' 'Thy belly', that is, thy will, is like a heap of wheat covered and compassed with lilies; for in the grains of wheat which form the bread of life, which thou now art tasting, the lilies of virtue, which gird thee about, fill thee with delight. For the daughters of the king, that is the virtues, will delight thee wondrously with the fragrance of their aromatical herbs, which are the knowledge of Himself which He gives thee. Thou wilt be so absorbed in this knowledge, and it will be so infused in thee, that thou shalt be also 'a well of living waters which run with a strong stream from Mount Libanus,' and Libanus is God. Thy joy will now be so marvellously complete, because the words of the Psalmist are accomplished in thee: 'The violence of the river maketh the city of God joyful.'

9. O wonder! The soul is now overflowing with the divine waters, which run from it as from an abundant fountain unto everlasting life.

It is true that this communication is light and fire of the lamps of God, yet the fire is here so sweet, that though an infinite fire, it is as the waters of life which satisfy the soul, and quench its thirst with that vehemence for which the spirit longs. Thus, though they are lamps of fire, they are also the living waters of the spirit. Those which descended on the Apostles, though lamps of fire, were also waters pure and limpid, according to the words of Ezechiel who thus prophesied the descent of the Holy Ghost: 'I will pour out upon you clean water, and will put a new spirit in the midst of you.' Thus though it be fire, it is water also, a figure of which we have in the sacrificial fire, hid by Jeremias, it was water in the place of concealment, but fire when it was brought forth and sprinkled upon the sacrifice.

10. So in like manner the Spirit of God, while hidden in the veins of the soul, is sweet water quenching its spiritual thirst; but when the soul offers the sacrifice of love, the Spirit is then living flames of fire, and these are the lamps of the acts of love which the bride spoke of in the Canticle when she said, 'The lamps thereof lamps of fire and flames.' The soul speaks of them thus because it has the fruition thereof not only as waters of wisdom, but also as the fire of love in an act of love, saying, 'O lamps of fire.' All language now is ineffectual to express the matter. If we consider that the soul is now transformed in God, we shall in some measure understand how it is true that it is also become a fountain of living waters boiling and bubbling upwards in the fire of love which is God.

In the splendours

11. I have already said that these splendours are the communications of the divine lamps in which the soul in union shines with its powers, memory, understanding, and will, enlightened and united in this loving knowledge. But we are not to suppose that the light of these splendours is like that of material fire, when it breaks into flames and heats objects external to it, but rather when it heats what is within it, for the soul is now within these splendours – 'in the splendours'. That is to say, it is within them, not near them, within

their splendours, in the flames of the lamps, itself transformed in flame.

12. The soul therefore may be said to resemble the air which is burning within the flame and transformed in fire, for the flame is nothing else but air inflamed. The flickerings of the flame are not those of air only or of fire only, but of air and fire together; and the fire causes the air which is within to burn. It is thus that the soul with its powers is illumined in the splendours of God. The movements of the flame, that is its vibrations and its flickerings, are not the work of the soul only, transformed in the fire of the Holy Ghost, nor of the Holy Ghost only, but of the soul and of the Holy Ghost together Who moves the soul as the fire moves the air that is burning.

13. Thus, then, these movements of God and of the soul together are as it were the acts of God by which He renders the soul glorious. For these vibrations and movements are the 'playing' and the joyous feasts of the Holy Ghost in the soul, spoken of before, in which He seems to be on the point of admitting it into everlasting life. And thus these movements and quiverings of the flame are as it were goads applied to the soul, furthering its translation into His perfect glory now that it is really entered into Him. So with fire: all movements and vibrations which it makes in the air burning within it, are efforts to ascend to its proper sphere, and that as quickly as possible, but they are all fruitless because the air itself is within its own sphere.

14. In the same way the movements of the Holy Ghost, though full of fire and most effectual to absorb the soul in great bliss, do not accomplish their work until the time is come when it is to sally forth from the sphere of the air of this mortal life and reach the centre of the spirit, the perfect life in Christ. These visions of the glory of God, to which the soul is now admitted, are more continuous than they used to be, more perfect and more stable; but in the life to come they will be most perfect, unchanging, and uninterrupted. There, too, the soul will see clearly how that God, though here appearing to move within it, yet in Himself moves not at all, as the fire moves not in its sphere. These splendours are inestimable graces and favours

which God bestows upon the soul. They are called also overshadow-ings, and are, in my opinion, the greatest and the highest graces which can be bestowed in this life in the way of transformation.

15. Now overshadowing is the throwing of a shadow; and to throw one's shadow over another signifies protection and favour, for when the shadow of one touches us, it is a sign that he whose shadow it is stands by us to favour and protect us. Thus it was said to the Virgin, 'The power of the Most High shall overshadow thee,' for the Holy Ghost was about to approach her so closely as to 'come upon' her. The shadow of every object partakes of the nature and proportions of it, for if the object be dense, the shadow will be dense and dark; if it be light and clear, so will be the shadow, as we see in the case of wood or crystal: the former being dense, throws a dark shadow, and the latter being clear, throws a shadow that is light. In spiritual things, too, death is the privation of all things, so the shadow of death will be darkness, which in a manner deprives us of all things. Thus, too, speaks the Psalmist, saying, 'sitting in darkness and the shadow of death', whether the spiritual darkness of spiritual death, or the bodily darkness of bodily death.

16. The shadow of life is light, if divine, a divine light, and if the shadow be human, the light is natural, and so the shadow of beauty will be as another beauty according to the nature and properties of that beauty of which it is the shadow. The shadow of strength will be as another strength, in measure and proportion. The shadow of wisdom will be another wisdom, or rather, beauty, strength, and wisdom themselves will be in the shadow, wherein is traced the form and property, the shadow whereof is there.

17. This, then, being so, what must be the shadow of the Holy Ghost, the shadow of all His power, might, and attributes, when He is so near the soul? He touches the soul not with His shadow only, for He unites Himself to it, feeling and tasting with it the form and attributes of God in the shadow of God: that is, feeling and tasting the property of divine power in the shadow of omnipotence: feeling and tasting the divine wisdom in the shadow of the divine wisdom: and finally, tasting the glory of God in the shadow of glory, which

begets the knowledge and the taste of the property and form of the glory of God. All this takes place in clear and luminous shadows, because the attributes and powers of God are lamps, which, being resplendent and luminous in their own nature, throw forth shadows resplendent and luminous, and a multitude of them in one sole essence.

18. O what a vision for the soul when it shall experience the power of that which Ezechiel saw: 'the likeness of four living creatures,' and the 'wheel with four faces', the appearance 'like that of burning coals of fire, and like the appearance of lamps'; when it shall behold that wheel, the wisdom of God, full of eyes within and without, that is the marvellous knowledge of wisdom; when it shall hear the noise of their wings as they pass, a noise 'like the noise of an army', that is of many things at once which the soul learns by one sole sound of God's passing before it; and finally, when it shall hear the beating of the wings, which is like the 'noise of many waters, as it were the voice of the Most High God', which signifies the rushing of the divine waters, the overflowing of which on the descent of the Holy Ghost envelops the soul in a flame of love. Here the soul rejoices in the glory of God, under the protection of His shadow, for the prophet adds: 'This was the vision of the likeness of the glory of our Lord.' O the height to which this blessed soul is raised! O how exalted! O how it marvels at the visions it has within the limits of the faith! Who can describe them? O how it is profoundly immersed in these waters of the divine splendours where the everlasting Father is pouring forth the irrigating streams with a bounteous hand, for these streams penetrate soul and body.

19. O wonder! the lamps of the divine attributes, though one in substance, are still distinct, each burning as the other, one being substantially the other. O abyss of delights, and the more abundant, the more their riches are gathered together in infinite simplicity and unity. There each one is so recognized and felt as not to hinder the feeling and recognition of the other; yea, rather everything in Thee is light which does not impede anything; and by reason of Thy pureness, O divine Wisdom, many things are known in Thee in one,

for Thou art the treasury of the everlasting Father, 'the brightness of eternal light, the unspotted mirror of God's majesty, and the image of His goodness', 'in the splendours'.

The deep caverns of sense,

20. The caverns are the powers of the soul, memory, understanding, and will, and their depth is commensurate with their capacity for great good, because nothing less than the infinite can fill them. What they suffer when they are empty, shows in some measure the greatness of their delight when they are full of God; for contraries are known by contraries. In the first place, it is to be remembered that these caverns are not conscious of their extreme emptiness when they are not purified and cleansed from all affection for created things. In this life every trifle that enters them is enough to perplex them, to render them insensible to their loss, and unable to recognize the infinite good which is wanting, or their own capacity for it. It is assuredly a most wonderful thing how, notwithstanding their capacity for infinite good, a mere trifle perplexes them, so that they cannot become the recipients of that for which they are intended, till they are completely emptied.

21. But when they are empty and cleansed, the hunger, the thirst, and the anxiety of the spiritual sense become intolerable, for as the appetite of these caverns is large, so their suffering is great, because the food which they need is great, namely, God. This feeling of pain, so deep, usually occurs towards the close of the illumination and the purgation of the soul, previous to the state of perfect union, during which it is satisfied. For when the spiritual appetite is empty, pure from every creature and from every affection thereto, and when the natural temper is lost and the soul attempered to the divine, and the emptied appetite is well disposed – the divine communication in the union with God being still withheld – the pain of this emptiness and thirst is greater than that of death, especially then when certain glimpses of the divine ray are visible, but not communicated. Souls in this state suffer from impatient love, and they cannot endure it long without either receiving that which

they desire, or dying.

22. As to the first cavern, which is the understanding, its emptiness is the thirst after God. So great is this thirst, that the Psalmist compares it to that of the hart, for he knew of none greater, saying, 'As the hart desireth the fountains of waters: so doth my soul desire Thee, O God.' This thirst is a thirst for the waters of the divine Wisdom, the object of the understanding. The second cavern is the will, and the emptiness thereof is a hunger so great after God, that the soul faints away, as the Psalmist saith, 'My soul longeth and fainteth for the courts of our Lord.' This hunger is for the perfection of love, the object of the soul's desires. The third cavern is the memory, and the emptiness thereof is the soul's melting away and languishing for the possession of God: 'I will be mindful and remember,' saith Jeremias, 'and my soul shall languish within me: these things I shall think over in my heart, therefore will I hope.'

23. Great, then, is the capacity of these caverns, because that which they are capable of containing is great and infinite, that is, God. Thus their capacity is in a certain sense infinite, their hunger and thirst infinite also, and their languishing and their pain, in their way, infinite. So when the soul is suffering this pain, though the pain be not so keen as in the other world, it seems to be a vivid image of that pain, because the soul is in a measure prepared to receive that which fills it, the privation of which is the greatest pain. Nevertheless the suffering belongs to another condition, for it abides in the depth of the will's love; but in this life love does not alleviate the pain, because the greater it is the greater the soul's impatience for the fruition of God, for which it hopes continually with intense desire.

24. But, O my God, seeing it is certain that when the soul truly longs for God it is already, as St Gregory saith, entered into possession, how comes it that it is in pain? If the desire of the angels, of which St Peter speaks, to look upon the Son of God is free from pain and anxiety, because they have the fruition of Him, it would seem then that the soul also having the fruition of God in proportion to its desire of Him – and the fruition of God is the fullness of delight –

must in this its desire, in proportion to its intensity, be conscious of that fullness, seeing that it longs so earnestly after God, and so herein there ought not to be any suffering or pain.

25. But it is not so, for there is a great difference between the fruition of God by grace only, and the fruition of Him in union; the former is one of mutual good will, the latter one of special communion. This difference resembles that which exists between betrothal and marriage. The former implies only an agreement and consent; bridal presents, and ornaments graciously given by the bridegroom. But marriage involves also personal union and mutual self-surrender. Though in the state of betrothal, the bridegroom is sometimes seen by the bride, and gives her presents; yet there is no personal union, which is the end of betrothal.

26. In the same way, when the soul has become so pure in itself, and in its powers, that the will is purged completely from all strange desires and inclinations, in its higher and lower nature, and is wholly given up to God, the will of both being one in free and ready concord, it has then attained to the fruition of God by grace in the state of betrothal and conformity of will. In this state of spiritual betrothal of the soul and the Word, The Bridegroom confers great favours upon the soul, and visits it oftentimes most lovingly to its great comfort and delight, but not to be compared with those of the spiritual marriage.

27. Now, though it is true that this takes place in the soul when it is perfectly cleansed of every affection to creatures – because that must occur previous to the spiritual betrothal – still other positive dispositions on the part of God, His visits and gifts of greater excellence, are requisite for this union, and for the spiritual marriage. It is by means of these dispositions, gifts, and visits, that the soul grows more and more in purity, beauty, and refinement, so as to be meetly prepared for a union so high. All this requires time, in some souls more, in others less. We have a type of this in the history of the virgins chosen for king Assuerus. These were taken in all the provinces of the kingdom, and brought from their fathers' houses; but before they could be presented to the king, they were kept in the palace a whole

year. For six months they were anointed with oil of myrrh, and for the other six with certain perfumes and sweet spices of a costlier nature, after which they appeared in the presence of the king.

28. During the time of the betrothal, and in expectation of the spiritual marriage in the unction of the Holy Ghost, when the unction disposing the soul for union is most penetrating, the anxieties of the caverns are wont to become most pressing and keen. For as these unctions are a proximate disposition for union with God, because most near unto Him, they make the soul more eager for Him, and inspire it with a keener longing after Him. Thus this desire is much more keen and deep, because the desire for God is a preparation for union with Him.

29. This is a good opportunity to warn souls whom God is guiding to this delicate unction to take care what they are doing, and to whose hands they commit themselves, that they may not go backwards, were it not beside my purpose. But such is the pain and grief of heart which I feel at the sight of some souls who go backwards, not only by withdrawing themselves from the further anointing of the Holy Ghost, but by losing the effects of what they have already received, that I cannot refrain from speaking on the subject, and telling them what they ought to do in order to avoid so great a loss. I will therefore leave my subject for a moment, but I shall return to it soon again. And in truth the consideration of this matter tends to elucidate the property of these caverns, and it is also necessary, not only for those souls who prosper in their work, but also for all others who are searching after the Beloved.

30. In the first place, if a soul is seeking after God, the Beloved is seeking it much more; if it sends after Him its loving desires, which are sweet as 'a pillar of smoke of aromatical spices, of myrrh and frankincense', He on His part sends forth the odour of His ointments, which draw the soul and make it run after Him. These ointments are His divine inspirations and touches, which if they come from Him, are always directed and ordered by the motives of perfection according to the law of God and the faith, in which perfection the soul must ever draw nearer and nearer unto God. The soul,

therefore, ought to see that the desire of God in all the graces which He bestows upon it by means of the unction and odour of His ointments, is to dispose it for another and higher unction, and more in union with His nature, until it attains to that simple and pure disposition, which is meritorious of the divine union, and of its transformation in all its powers.

31. The soul, therefore, considering that God is the chief doer in this matter, that it is He Who guides it and leads it by the hand whither it cannot come of itself, namely, unto supernatural things beyond the reach of understanding, memory, and will, must take especial care to put no difficulties in the way of its guide, Who is the Holy Ghost, on that road along which He leads it by the law of God and the faith. Such a difficulty will be raised if the soul intrusts itself to a blind guide; and the blind guides which can lead it astray are three, namely, the spiritual director, the devil, and its own self.

32. As to the first of these, it is of the greatest importance to the soul desirous of perfection and anxious not to fall back, to consider well into whose hands it resigns itself; for as the master so is the disciple; as the father so the child. You will scarcely find one who is in all respects qualified to guide a soul in the higher parts of this road, or even in the ordinary divisions of it, for a director must be learned, prudent and experienced. Though the foundations of good direction be learning and discretion, yet if experience of the higher ways be wanting, there are no means of guiding a soul therein when God is showing the way, and inexperienced directors may do great harm. Such directors, not understanding these ways of the Spirit, very frequently make souls lose the unction of the delicate ointments, by means of which the Holy Ghost is preparing them for Himself: they are guiding them by other means of which they have read, but which are adapted only for beginners. These directors, knowing how to guide beginners only — and God grant they may know that — will not suffer their penitents to advance, though it be the will of God, beyond the mere rudiments, acts of reflection and imagination, whereby their progress is extremely little.

33. In order to have a better knowledge of the state of beginners,

we must keep in mind that it is one of meditation and of acts of reflection. It is necessary to furnish the soul in this state with matter for meditation, that it may make reflections and interior acts, and avail itself of the sensible spiritual heat and fervour, for this is necessary in order to accustom the senses and desires to good things, that, being satisfied by the sweetness thereof, they may be detached from the world.

34. When this is in some degree effected, God begins at once to introduce the soul into the state of contemplation, and that very quickly, especially religious, because these, having renounced the world, quickly fashion their senses and desires according to God; they have therefore to pass at once from meditation to contemplation. This passage, then, takes place when the discursive acts and meditation fail, when sensible sweetness and first fervours cease, when the soul cannot make reflections as before, nor find any sensible comfort, but is fallen into aridity, because the chief matter is changed into the spirit, and the spirit is not cognizable by sense. As all the natural operations of the soul, which are within its control, depend on the senses only, it follows that God is now working in a special manner in this state, that it is He that infuses and teaches, that the soul is the recipient on which He bestows spiritual blessings by contemplation, the knowledge and the love of Himself together; that is, He gives it loving knowledge without the instrumentality of its discursive acts, because it is no longer able to form them as before.

35. At this time, then, the direction of the soul must be wholly different from what it was at first. If formerly it was supplied with matter for meditation and it did meditate, now that matter must be withheld and meditation must cease, because, as I have said, it cannot meditate, do what it will, and distractions are the result. If before it looked for fervour and sweetness and found them, let it look for them no more nor desire them; and if it attempt to seek them, not only will it not find them, but it will meet with aridity, because it turns away from the peaceful and tranquil good secretly bestowed upon it, when it attempts to fall back on the operations of sense. In

this way it loses the latter without gaining the former, because the senses have ceased to be the channel of spiritual good.

36. Souls in this state are not to be forced to meditate or to apply themselves to discursive reflections laboriously effected, neither are they to strive after sweetness and fervour, for if they did so, they would be thereby hindering the principal agent, Who is God Himself, for He is now secretly and quietly infusing wisdom into the soul, together with the loving knowledge of Himself, without many divers distinct or separated acts. But He produces them sometimes in the soul, and that for some space of time. The soul then must be lovingly intent upon God without distinctly eliciting other acts beyond these to which He inclines it; it must be as it were passive, making no efforts of its own, purely, simply, and lovingly intent upon God, as a man who opens his eyes with loving attention. For as God is now dealing with the soul in the way of bestowing by simple and loving knowledge, so the soul also, on its part, must deal with Him in the way of receiving by simple and loving knowledge, so that knowledge may be joined to knowledge, and love to love; because it is necessary here that the recipient should be adapted to the gift, and not otherwise, and that the gift may be accepted and preserved as it is given.

37. It is evident, therefore, that if the soul does not now abandon its ordinary way of meditation, it will receive this gift of God in a scanty and imperfect manner, not in that perfection with which it is bestowed; for the gift being so grand, and an infused gift, cannot be received in this scanty and imperfect way. Consequently, if the soul will at this time make efforts of its own, and encourage another disposition than that of passive loving attention, most submissive and calm, and if it does not abstain from its previous discursive acts, it will place a barrier against those graces which God is about to communicate to it in this loving knowledge. He gives His grace to beginners in the exercise of purgation, as I have said, and afterwards with an increase of the sweetness of love.

38. But if the soul is to be the recipient of His grace passively, in the natural way of God, and not in the supernatural way of the soul,

it follows that, in order to be such a recipient, it must be perfectly detached, calm, peaceful, and serene, as God is; it must be like the atmosphere, which the sun illumines and warms in proportion to its calmness and purity. Thus the soul must be attached to nothing, not even to meditation, not to sensible or spiritual sweetness, because God requires a spirit free and annihilated, for every act of the soul, even of thought, of liking or disliking, will hinder and disturb it, and break that profound silence of sense and spirit necessary for hearing the deep and soft voice of God, Who, in the words of Osee, speaks to the heart in solitude; it is in profound peace and tranquillity that the soul, like David, is to listen to God, Who will speak peace unto His people. When this takes place, when the soul feels that it is silent and listens, its loving attention must be most pure, without a thought of self, in a manner self-forgotten, so that it shall be wholly intent upon hearing, for thus it is that the soul is free and ready for that which our Lord requires at its hands.

39. This tranquillity and self-forgetfulness are ever attended with a certain interior absorption; and, therefore, under no circumstances whatever, either of time or place, is it lawful for the soul, now that it has begun to enter the state of contemplation, tranquil and simple, to recur to its previous meditation, or to cleave to spiritual sweetness, as I have said, and at great length, in the tenth chapter of the first book of *The Dark Night*, and previously in the last chapter of the second, and in the first of the third book of *The Ascent of Mount Carmel*. It must detach itself from all spiritual sweetness, rise above it in freedom of spirit; this is what the prophet Habacuc did, for he says of himself, 'I will stand upon my watch' over my senses – that is, I will leave them below – 'and fix my step upon the munition' of my faculties – that is, they shall not advance a step even in thought – ' and I will behold to see what will be said to me,' that is, I will receive what God shall communicate to me passively.

40. I have already said that to contemplate is to receive, and it is impossible to receive the highest wisdom, that is contemplation, otherwise than in a silent spirit, detached from all sweetness and particular knowledge. So the Prophet Isaias when he says, 'Whom

shall He teach knowledge? and whom shall He make to understand the thing heard? them that are weaned from the milk,' that is from sweetness and personal likings, 'that are plucked away from the breasts,' from reliance on particular knowledge. Take away, O spiritual man, the mote and the film from thine eye, and make it clean, and then the sun will shine for thee, and thou shalt see clearly, establish thy soul in the freedom of calm peace, withdraw it from the yoke and slavery of the miserable efforts of thine own strength, which is the captivity of Egypt – for all thou canst do is little more than to gather straw for the bricks – and guide it into the land of promise flowing with milk and honey.

41. O spiritual director, remember it is for this liberty and holy rest of sons that God calls the soul into the wilderness; there it journeys in festal robes, with ornaments of gold and silver, for the Egyptians are spoiled and their riches carried away. Nor is this all: the enemies of the soul are drowned in the sea of contemplation, where the Egyptian of sense finds no support for his feet, leaving the child of God free, that is the spirit, to transcend the narrow limits of its own operations, of its low views, rude perceptions, and wretched likings. God does all this for the soul that He may give it the sweet manna, which, though 'it contains all that is delicious and the sweetness of every taste' – objects of desire for the soul according to thy direction – and though it is so delicious that it melts in the mouth, thy penitent shall not taste of it, if he desires anything else, for he shall not receive it.

42. Strive, therefore, to root out of the soul all desire of consolation, sweetness, and meditations; do not disquiet it about spiritual things, still less about earthly things; establish it in perfect detachment, and in the utmost possible solitude. For the greater its progress in this, and the more rapidly it attains to this calm tranquillity, the more abundant will be the infusion of the spirit of divine wisdom, the loving, calm, lonely, peaceful, sweet ravisher of the spirit. The soul will feel itself at times enraptured, gently and tenderly wounded, not knowing by whom, how, or when, because the Spirit communicates Himself to it without effort on its part. The

least work of God in the soul in this state of holy rest and solitude is an inestimable good, transcending the very thought of the soul and of its spiritual guide, and though it does not appear so then, it will show itself in due time.

43. What the soul is now conscious of is a certain estrangement and alienation from all things around it, at one time more than at another, with a certain sweet aspiration of love and life of the spirit, an inclination to solitude, and a sense of weariness in the things of this world, for when we taste of the spirit, the flesh becomes insipid. But the interior goods which silent contemplation impresses on the soul without the soul's consciousness of them, are of inestimable value, for they are the most secret and delicious unctions of the Holy Ghost, whereby He secretly fills the soul with the riches of His gifts and graces; for being God, He doeth the work of God as God.

44. These goods, then, these great riches, these sublime and delicate unctions, this knowledge of the Holy Ghost, which, on account of their exquisite and subtile pureness, neither the soul itself, nor he who directs it, can comprehend, but only He Who infuses them in order to render it more pleasing to Himself — are most easily, even by the slightest application of sense or desire to any particular knowledge or sweetness, disturbed and hindered. This is a serious evil, grievous and lamentable. O how sad and how wonderful! The evil done is not perceived, and the barrier raised between God and the soul is almost nothing, and yet it is more grievous, an object of deeper sorrow, and inflicts a greater stain, than any other, though seemingly more important, in common souls which have not attained to such a high state of pureness. It is as if a beautiful painting were roughly handled, besmeared with coarse and vile colours; for the injury done is greater, more observable, and more deplorable, than it would be if a multitude of common paintings were thus bedaubed.

45. Though this evil be so great that it cannot be exaggerated, it is still so common that there is scarcely one spiritual director who does not inflict it upon souls whom God has begun to lead by this way to contemplation. For, whenever God is anointing a soul with the

unction of loving knowledge, most delicate, serene, peaceful, lonely, strange to sense and imagination; whenever He withholds all sweetness from it, and suspends its power of meditation – because He reserves it for this lonely unction, inclining it to solitude and quiet – a spiritual director will appear, who, like a rough blacksmith, knows only the use of his hammer, and who, because all his knowledge is limited to the coarser work, will say to it: Come, get rid of this, this is waste of time and idleness: arise and meditate, resume thine interior acts, for it is necessary that thou shouldest make diligent efforts of thine own; everything else is delusion and folly. Such a director as this does not understand the degrees of prayer, nor the ways of the Spirit, neither does he consider that what he recommends the soul to do is already done, since it has passed beyond meditation and is detached from the things of sense; for when the goal is reached, and the journey ended, all further travelling must be away from the goal.

46. Such a director, therefore, is one who understands not that the soul has already attained to the life of the Spirit, wherein there is no reflection, and where the senses cease from their work; where God is Himself the agent in a special way, and is speaking in secret to the solitary soul. Directors of this kind bedaub the soul with the coarse ointments of particular knowledge and sensible sweetness, to which they bring it back; they rob it of its loneliness and recollection, and consequently disfigure the exquisite work which God was doing within it. The soul that is under such guidance as this fails in one method and does not profit by the other.

47. Let spiritual directors of this kind remember, that the Holy Ghost is the principal agent here, and the real guide of souls; that He never ceases to take care of them and never neglects any means by which they may profit and draw near unto God as quickly as possible, and in the best way. Let them remember that they are not the agents, but instruments only to guide souls by the rule of the faith and law of God, according to the spirit which God gives to every one. Their aim therefore should be, not to guide souls by a way of their own suitable to themselves, but to ascertain, if they can, the way by which God Himself is guiding them. If they cannot ascertain

it, let them leave these souls alone and not disquiet them. Let them adapt their instructions to the direction of God, and endeavour to lead their penitents into greater solitude, liberty, and tranquillity, and not fetter them when God is leading them on.

48. The spiritual director must not be anxious or afflicted because the soul is doing nothing, as he imagines, for provided the soul of his penitent be detached from all particular knowledge, from every desire and inclination of sense; provided it abide in the self-denial of poverty of spirit, emptied of darkness and sweetness, weaned from the breast – for this is all that the soul should look to, and all that the spiritual director is to consider as within the province of them both – it is impossible – according to the course of the divine goodness and mercy – that God will not perform His own work, yea, more impossible than that the sun should not shine in a clear and cloudless sky. As the sun rising in the morning enters the house if the windows are open, so God, the unsleeping keeper of Israel, enters the emptied soul and fills it with good things. God is, like the sun, above our souls and ready to enter within them.

49. Let spiritual directors, therefore, be content to prepare souls according to the laws of evangelical perfection, which consists in detachment, and in the emptiness of sense and spirit. Let them not go beyond this with the building, for that is the work of our Lord alone, from Whom cometh 'every perfect gift'. For, 'unless our Lord build the house, they labour in vain that build it.' And as He is the supernatural builder, He will build up in every soul, according to His own good pleasure, the supernatural building. Do thou, who art the spiritual director, dispose the natural faculties by annihilating them in their acts – that is thy work; the work of God, as the Wise Man says, is to direct man's steps towards supernatural goods by ways and means utterly unknown to thee and thy penitent.

50. Say not, therefore, that thy penitent is making no progress, or is doing nothing, for if he have no greater pleasure than he once had in particular knowledge, he is advancing towards that which is above nature. Neither do thou complain that thy penitent has no distinct perceptions, for if he had he would be making no progress, because

God is incomprehensible, surpassing all understanding. And so the further the penitent advances, the further from himself must he go, walking by faith, believing and not seeing; he thus draws nearer unto God by not understanding, than by understanding. Trouble not thyself about this, for if the understanding goes not backwards occupying itself with distinct knowledge and other matters of this world, it is going forwards; for to go forwards is to go more and more by faith. The understanding, having neither the knowledge nor the power of comprehending God, advances towards Him by not understanding. Thus, then, what thou judgest amiss in thy penitent is for his profit: namely, that he does not perplex himself with distinct perceptions, but walks onwards in perfect faith.

51. Or, you will say, perhaps, that the will, if the understanding have no distinct perceptions, will be at the least idle, and without love, because we can love nothing that we do not know. That is true as to the natural actions of the soul, for the will does not love or desire anything of which there is no distinct conception in the understanding. But in the matter of infused contemplation, it is not at all necessary for the soul to have distinct knowledge, or to form many discursive acts, because God Himself is then communicating to it loving knowledge, which is at the same time heat and light indistinctly, and then according to the state of the understanding love also is in the will. As the knowledge is general and dim – the understanding being unable to conceive distinctly what it understands – so the will also loves generally and indistinctly. For as God is light and love in this delicate communication, He informs equally the understanding and the will, though at times His presence is felt in one more than in the other. At one time the understanding is more filled with knowledge than the will with love, and at another, love is deeper than knowledge.

52. There is no reason, therefore, to be afraid of the will's idleness in this state, for if it ceases to elicit acts directed by particular knowledge, so far as they depend on itself, God inebriates it with infused love through the knowledge which contemplation ministers, as I have just said.

53. These acts of the will which are consequent upon infused

contemplation are so much the nobler, the more meritorious and the sweeter, the nobler the source, God, Who infuses this love and kindles it in the soul, for the will is now near unto God, and detached from other joys. Take care, therefore, to empty the will and detach it from all its inclinations, for if it is not going backwards, searching after sweetness and comfort, even though it have none in God distinctly felt, it is really advancing upwards above all such things to God, seeing that it is without any particular pleasure.

54. And though the penitent have no particular comfort in God distinctly apprehended, though he does not make distinct acts of love, he does find more comfort in Him in that general secret and dim infusion than if he were under the influence of distinct acts of knowledge, because the soul sees clearly then that not one of them can furnish so much comfort and delight as this calm and lonely infusion. He loves God, too, more than all lovely things, because the soul has thrown aside all other joys and pleasures; they have become insipid.

55. There is no ground for uneasiness here, for if the will can find no rest in the joys and satisfactions of particular acts, there is then real progress, because not to go backwards, embracing what is sensible, is to go onwards to the unapproachable, Who is God. Hence, then, if the will is to advance, it is to do so more by detachment from, than by attachment to, what is pleasurable and sweet. Herein is fulfilled the precept of love, namely, that we are to love Him above all things. And if this love is to be perfect, we must live in perfect detachment, and in a special emptiness of all things.

56. Neither are we to be distressed when the memory is emptied of all forms and figures; for as God is without form or figure, the memory is safe when emptied of them, and draws thereby the nearer to God. For the more the memory relies on the imagination, the further it departs from God, and the greater the risks it runs; because God, being above our thoughts, is not cognizable by the imagination. These spiritual directors, not understanding souls who have already entered into the state of quiet and solitary contemplation, because they know it not, and perhaps have never advanced

beyond the ordinary state of reflection and meditation themselves, look upon the penitents, of whom I am speaking, as idle – for 'the sensual man', the man who still dwells with the feelings of the sensual part of the soul, 'perceiveth not these things that are of the Spirit of God' – disturb the peace of that calm and tranquil contemplation given them by God, and force them back to their former meditations.

57. This is followed by great loss, repugnance, dryness, and distractions on the part of penitents, who desire to abide in quiet and peaceful self-recollection. These directors will have them strive after sweetness and fervours, though in truth they should have given them a wholly different advice. The penitents are unable to follow their direction, being incapable of meditating as before; because the time for that is past, and because that is not their road. They are, therefore, doubly disquieted, and imagine themselves in the way of perdition. Their directors encourage them in this supposition, dry up their spirit, rob them of the precious unctions which God gave them in solitude and calm – and this is a great evil – and furnish them with mere mud instead, for they lose the former, and labour in vain with the latter.

58. Such directors as these do not really know what spirituality is. They wrong God most grievously, and treat Him irreverently, putting forth their coarse hands to the work which He is doing Himself. It has cost God not a little to have brought souls thus far, and He greatly prizes this solitude to which He has led them, this emptiness of their faculties, for He has brought them thither that He may speak to their heart, that is what He always desires. He is now taking them by the hand, and reigning in them in the abundance of peace. He has deprived the discursive faculties of their strength, wherewith they had 'laboured all the night' and had taken nothing. He feeds them now in spirit, not by the operation of sense, because the senses together with their acts cannot contain the spirit.

59. How precious in His sight is this calm, or sleep, or annihilation of the senses, His words in the Canticle show: 'I adjure you, O daughters of Jerusalem, by the roes and harts of the fields, that you

stir not up nor awake my beloved till she please.' Those words tell us how much He loves this sleep and lonely oblivion of the soul, by the mention of those solitary and retiring animals. But the spiritual directors of whom I am speaking will not suffer their penitents to rest, they insist upon continual labour, so that God shall find no opportunity for doing His work; the work of God they undo and disfigure by the work of the soul, and the little foxes that destroy the vines are not driven away. God complains of these directors by the mouth of the Prophet, saying, 'You have devoured the vineyard.'

60. But it may be said that these directors err, perhaps, with good intentions, because their knowledge is scanty. Be it so; but they are not therefore justified in giving the rash counsels they do, without previously ascertaining the way and spirit of their penitent. And if they do not understand the matter, it is not for them to interfere in what they do not comprehend, but rather to leave their penitent to others who understand him better than they. It is not a light fault to cause by a wrong direction the loss of inestimable blessings, and to endanger a soul. Thus, he who rashly errs, being under an obligation to give good advice — for so is every one in the office he assumes — shall not go unpunished for the evil he has done. The affairs of God are to be handled with great caution and watchful circumspection, and especially this, which is so delicate, and so high, and where the gain is infinite if the direction given be right, and the loss also infinite if it be wrong.

61. But if you say that such a director may be excused — though for my part I do not see how — you must at least admit that he is inexcusable who keeps a penitent in his power for certain empty reasons and considerations known only to himself: he will not go unpunished. It is quite certain that a soul which is to make progress in the spiritual life, and which God is ever helping, must change its method of prayer, and be in need of a higher direction and of another spirit than those of such a director. Not all directors have the knowledge which every event on the spiritual road requires; neither are they all qualified to determine how a given soul is to be directed under every circumstance of the spiritual life; at least they must not

presume that they are, or that it is God's will that a particular soul shall not advance further. As it is not everyone who can trim a block of wood, can also carve an image out of it; nor can everyone form the outlines who can carve; nor can everyone who fashions the outlines paint them, as neither can everyone who can paint perfect and complete the image: for everyone of these can do only what he understands himself; and if any one of them were to attempt that which is not within the compass of his skill, he would spoil the statue.

62. So is it in the spiritual life; for if a director whose only work it is to trim the rude block, that is, to make his penitent despise the world, and mortify his desires; or if, further, it be that of the carver, who is to guide the soul into holy meditations, and his science extend no further, how can he guide his penitent to the highest perfection of the finished portrait, to that delicate colouring which consists not in the rough hewing of the wood, nor in the carving thereof, nor even in the formation of the outlines, but is rather a work which God Himself perfects in the soul with His own hand? It is therefore quite certain that such a director as this, whose teaching is ever the same, cannot help driving back the penitent whom he subjects to it, or, at the least, hindering his advancement. For what will be the state of the image, if nothing be done to it but to rough-hew the wood and beat it with a mallet? What is this, but the discipline of the faculties? When shall the image be finished? When shall it be ready for God to colour it?

63. Is it possible that any spiritual director can think himself qualified for all this? that he looks upon himself as sufficiently skilful, so as to render the teaching of another needless for his penitent? Granting even that he is qualified for the whole direction of a particular soul, because, perhaps, such a soul has no vocation for a higher walk, it is almost impossible that he can be also a sufficient guide for all whom he hinders from passing out of his hands into the hands of others. God leads every soul by a separate path, and you will scarcely meet with one spirit which agrees with another in one half of the way by which it advances. Who can be like St Paul, who

'became all things to all men, that he might save all'?

64. Thou art thus become a tyrant of souls, the robber of their liberties, claiming for thyself all the freedom of the evangelical doctrine, and taking care that none of thy penitents leave thee; yea, still further, and much worse, should it come to thy knowledge that any of them had gone elsewhere for direction, or to discuss a question which it was not convenient to submit to thee; or if God had led them for the purpose of learning what thou teachest not – I say it with shame – thou art jealous, like a husband of his wife. This is not zeal for the honour of God, but the zeal which cometh out of thine own pride and presumption. How couldest thou be sure that thy penitent had no need of other guidance than thine? With such directors God is angry and he threatens to chastise them, saying: 'Woe to the shepherds of Israel . . . you eat the milk and you clothed yourself with the wool . . . but my flock you did not feed . . . I will require my flock at their hand.'

65. These directors, therefore, ought to leave their penitents at liberty, yea, they lie under an obligation to allow them to have recourse to the advice of others, and always to receive them again with a cheerful countenance; for they know not by what way God intends to lead them, especially when their present direction is not suited to them. That, indeed, is a sign that God is leading their penitents by another road, and that they require another director; they should, therefore, counsel the change, for a contrary course of proceeding springs from a foolish pride and presumption.

66. Let me now pass on from this and speak of other means, fatal as the plague, which these directors, or others worse than they, make use of in the guidance of souls. When God sends into a soul the unctions of holy desires, and leads it to give up the world, draws it on to change its state of life, and to serve Him by despising the world – it is a great matter in His eyes that souls should have advanced to this, for the things of the world are not according to the heart of God – these directors, with their human reasonings and worldly motives, contrary to the doctrine of Christ, at variance with mortification and contempt of all things, consulting their own interest or pleasure, or fearing where no

fear is, interpose delays or suggest difficulties, or, what is worse, take away all such good thoughts from the hearts of their penitents. These directors have an evil spirit, are indevout and exceedingly worldly; unaccustomed to the ways of Christ, they do not enter in themselves by the strait gate, neither will they suffer others to enter. These are they whom our Lord threatens in the Gospel, saying: 'Woe to you lawyers, for you have taken away the key of knowledge: you yourselves have not entered in, and those that were entering you have hindered.'

67. These directors are in truth like barriers before the gate of heaven, forgetting that God has called them to the functions they exercise that they may compel those to enter in whom He has invited. He has given them this charge in the Gospel, but they, on the contrary, compel their penitents not to enter in by the narrow gate which leadeth unto life. Such a director as this is one of the blind guides who thwarts the direction of the Holy Ghost. This happens in many ways; some err knowingly; others ignorantly; but both the one and the other shall be punished; for by taking upon themselves the office which they fill, they are bound to understand and consider what they do.

68. The other blind guide that disturbs the soul in this interior recollection is Satan, who, being blind himself, desires to render the soul blind also. He labours, therefore, when the soul has entered into those deep solitudes, wherein the delicate unctions of the Holy Ghost are infused – he hates and envies the soul for this, because he sees it fly beyond his reach, adorned with the riches of God – to throw over the soul's detachment and estrangement from the world, certain cataracts of knowledge, and the darkness of sensible sweetness, sometimes good, the more to entice the soul, and to draw it back to the way of sense. He would have it fix its eyes on this, and make use of it with a view of drawing near to God, relying upon this kind of knowledge, and sensible sweetness. By this means Satan distracts the soul, and easily withdraws it from that solitude and recollection wherein the Holy Ghost worketh secretly His great marvels within.

69. And then the soul, naturally prone to sensible satisfactions

and sweetness – especially if it aims at them – is most easily led to rely upon such knowledge and sweetness, and so draws back from the solitude wherein God was working. For as the soul, as it seemed, was doing nothing then, this new way appears preferable, because it is something, while solitude seemed to be nothing. How sad it is that the soul, not understanding its own state, should, for one mouthful, disqualify itself from feeding upon God Himself; for He offers Himself to be its food when He absorbs it in these spiritual and solitary unctions of His mouth.

70. In this way, the evil spirit, for a mere nothing, inflicts upon souls the very greatest injuries, causing the loss of great riches, and dragging them forth, like fish with a trifling bait, out of the depths of the pure waters of the spirit, where they were engulfed and drowned in God, resting upon no created support. He drags them to the bank, and supplies them with objects whereon to rest, and makes them walk on the earth painfully, that they may not float on 'the waters of Siloe, that run with silence,' bathed in the unctions of God. It is wonderful how much Satan makes of this: and as a slight injury inflicted on the soul in this state is a great one, you will scarcely meet with one which has gone this way that has not suffered great injuries, and incurred grievous losses. Satan stations himself with great cunning on the frontiers between sense and spirit; there he deludes the soul, and feeds the senses, interposing sensible things to keep it back, and hinder it from escaping out of his hands.

71. The soul, too, is most easily taken by these devices, for it knows as yet of nothing better; neither does it dream that this is a loss, yea, rather, it looks on it as a great gain, and accepts the suggestions of the evil one gladly, for it thinks that God has come to visit it; consequently it omits to enter into the inner chamber of the Bridegroom, and stands at the door to see what is passing without in the sensual part of itself.

72. The devil, in the words of Job, 'seeth every high thing' that relates to souls that he may assail them. If, therefore, a soul becomes recollected, he labours to disturb it by horrors and fears, or by bodily pains, or outward noise and tumults, that he may ruin it; he strives to

draw its attention to the tumult he excites, and to fix it upon what is passing without, and to withdraw it from the interior spirit, but when he fails in his efforts he leaves it alone. So easily does Satan squander great riches and bring about the ruin of these precious souls, though he thinks this of more consequence than the fall of many others, that he looks upon it as a small matter because of the ease with which he effects it and because of the little trouble it costs him.

73. We may also understand in the same sense the following words spoken by God to Job: 'Lo! he shall sop up the river and shall not marvel: and he hath confidence that Jordan' – the highest perfection – 'may run into his mouth. In his eyes as with a hook he shall take him, and with stakes he shall bore through his nostrils.' That is, he will turn away the soul from true spirituality by means of the arrows of distinct knowledge wherewith he pierces it, for the breath which goeth out through the nostrils in one volume becomes dispersed if the nostrils be pierced, and escapes through the divers perforations.

74. Again it is said, 'The beams of the sun shall be under him, and he shall strew gold under as dirt.' He causes souls that have been enlightened to lose the marvellous beams of divine knowledge, takes away and disperses abroad the precious gold of the divine adorning by which souls had been made rich.

75. O souls, now that God shows you mercies so great, leading you into solitude and recollection, withdrawing you from the labours of sense, do not return thereto. If your own exertions were once profitable, enabling you to deny the world and your own selves when you were but beginners, cease from them now when God of His mercy has begun to work in you, for now they will only embarrass you. If you will be careful to lay no stress on your own operations, withdrawing them from all things, and involving them in nothing – which is your duty in your present state – and wait lovingly and sincerely upon God at the same time – doing no violence to yourselves except to detach yourselves wholly, so as not to disturb your tranquillity and peace – God Himself will feed you with the heavenly food, since you cease to hinder Him.

76. The third blind guide of the soul is the soul itself, which, not

understanding its own state, disturbs and injures itself. For as the soul knows of no operations except those of sense; when God leads it into solitude, where it cannot exert its faculties and elicit the acts it elicited before, and as it appears to itself then to be doing nothing, it strives to elicit its previous acts more distinctly and more sensibly. The consequence is distraction, dryness, and disgust in that very soul which once delighted in the calm peace and spiritual silence, wherein God Himself was in secret infusing His sweetness. It sometimes happens that God persists in keeping the soul in this quiet calm, and that the soul persists in crying out with the imagination, and in walking with the understanding. Such souls are like children in their mothers' arms, who, unable to walk, cry, and struggle with their feet, demanding to be allowed to walk alone, but who cannot walk themselves, and suffer not their mothers to do so either. These souls make God resemble a painter whose work is hindered because the subject he portrays will not be still.

77. The soul, then, should keep in mind that it is now making greater progress than it could make by any efforts of its own, though it be wholly unconscious of that progress. God Himself is carrying it in His own arms, and thus it happens that it is not aware that it is advancing. Though it thinks that it is doing nothing, yet in truth more is done than if itself were the agent; for God Himself is working. If this work be invisible, that is nothing strange, for the work of God in the soul is not cognizable by sense, because silently wrought: 'The words of the wise are heard in silence.' Let the soul abandon itself to the hands of God and trust in Him. He that will do so shall walk securely, for there is no danger then unless the soul should attempt anything in its own strength, or by the wilful exercise of its proper faculties.

78. Let us now return to the deep caverns of the senses, in which I said the sufferings of the soul are ordinarily very great when God is anointing it, and preparing it for union with Himself by His subtile and delicate unctions. These unctions of God are so subtile that, penetrating into the inmost depths of the soul, they so dispose it, and so fill it with sweetness, that the sufferings and fainting of the

soul through its great desire in the immense void of the caverns are immeasurable. Now if the unction which disposes the caverns for the union of the spiritual marriage be so wonderful, what shall the accomplishment thereof be? Certain it is that as the hunger and thirst and suffering of the caverns, so will be the satisfaction, fullness, and delight thereof. According to the perfection of these dispositions will be the delight of the fruition and possession of the sense of the soul, which is the power and energy of its very substance for perceiving and delighting in the objects of its faculties.

79. These faculties are with great propriety called caverns. For as the soul is conscious that they admit the profound intelligence and splendours of the lamps, it sees clearly also, that they are deep in proportion to the depth of the intelligence and love; that they have space and capacity commensurate with the distinct sources of the intelligence, of the sweetness and delight which it receives in them. All this is received and established in the cavern of the sense of the soul which is the capacity thereof for possession, perception, and fruition. Thus, as the common sense of the imagination is the place where all the objects of the outward senses are treasured up, so is this common sense of the soul enlightened and made rich by a possession so grand and so glorious.

Dim and dark,

80. The eye sees not for two reasons; either because it is in darkness or is blind. God is the light and the true object of the soul, and when He does not shine upon it, it is then in darkness, though its power of vision may be most perfect. When the soul is in sin, or when it occupies the desires with other things than God, it is then blind. Though the light of God be not wanted to it then, yet, being blind, it cannot see the light because of its blindness, which is the practical ignorance in which it lives. Before God enlightened the soul in its transformation it was in darkness and ignorant of His great goodness, as was the Wise Man before he was enlightened, for he says, 'He enlightened my ignorance.'

81. Speaking spiritually, it is one thing to be blind and another to

be in darkness. Blindness proceeds from sin, but darkness does not necessarily involve sin, and it happens in two ways. There is natural darkness where the light of natural things shines not, and there is supernatural darkness where there is no knowledge of many supernatural things. Here the soul says with regard to them both, that the understanding without God abode in darkness. For until our Lord said, 'Let light be,' darkness was upon the face of the deep of the cavern of the soul's sense. The deeper the cavern when God shines not upon it, the deeper is the darkness thereof. Thus it is impossible for it to lift up the eyes to the divine light, yea the divine light is not even thought of, because never seen or known to exist; there is therefore no desire for it. And the soul desires darkness rather than light, and so goes on from darkness to darkness, led by darkness, for darkness can lead only to darkness again.

82. David saith, 'day to day uttereth word and night to night showeth knowledge,' thus as the deep of darkness calleth another deep, and the deep of light another deep of light; like calling upon like, so the light of grace which God had before given to the soul, and by which He opened the eyes of it from the deep to behold the divine light, and made it pleasing to Himself, calls to another deep of grace, namely, the divine transformation of the soul in God, wherein the eye of sense is enlightened and rendered pleasing.

83. The eye was also blind in that it took pleasure in other than God. The blindness of the higher and rational sense is caused by the desire which, like a cloud or a cataract, overlies and covers the eye of reason, so that it shall not see what is before it. Thus, then, the grandeur and magnificence of the divine beauty are rendered invisible, so far as the pleasure of sense is followed. For if we cover the eye with anything, however trifling it may be, that is enough to obstruct the vision of objects before us be they ever so large. Thus, then, a single desire entertained by the soul suffices to hinder the vision of all the divine grandeurs which are higher than its desires and longings. Who can say how impossible it is for the soul, subject to desires, to judge of the things of God? for he that would judge aright of these must cast away all desires, because he cannot judge aright while

subject thereto; for in that case he will come to consider the things of God not to be God's, and those things which are not God's to be the things of God.

84. While this cloud and cataract cover the eye of the judgment, nothing is visible except the cloud, sometimes of one colour, sometimes of another, according to circumstances, and men will take the cloud for God, because they see nothing beside the cloud which overshadows the sense, and God is not comprehended by sense. Thus, desire and sensual satisfactions hinder the knowledge of high things, as it is written, 'The bewitching of vanity obscureth good things, and the inconstancy of concupiscence perverteth the understanding' that is without malice. Those persons, therefore, who are not so spiritual as to be purified from their desires and inclinations, but are still sensual, believe those things to be important which are in truth of no account in spirituality, being intimately connected with sense; they make no account of and despise the deep things of the spirit, which are further removed from sense, yea sometimes they look upon them as folly, as we learn from St Paul, 'The sensual man perceiveth not these things that are of the Spirit of God: for it is foolishness to him and he cannot understand.'

85. The sensual man is he who still lives according to the desires and inclinations of nature, and even though these desires come occasionally into contact with the things of the spirit, yet, if man cleaves to spiritual things with his natural desires, they are still natural desires only. The spirituality of the object is little to the purpose, if the desire of it proceed from itself, having its root and strength in nature. What! you will say, is it not a supernatural desire to desire God? No, not always; but only then when the motive is supernatural, and when the strength of the desire proceeds from God; that is a very different thing. When the desire comes from thyself, so far as it relates to the manner thereof, it is nothing more than natural. So, then, when thou art attached to thy spiritual tastes, exerting thine own natural desire, thou bringest a cataract over thine eye, thou art sensual, incapable of perceiving or judging what is spiritual, for that transcends all natural sense and desire.

86. If thou still doubtest, I have nothing further to add except to bid thee read over again what I have written, and that done perhaps the doubts will vanish. What I have said is the substance of the truth, and I cannot now enlarge upon it. The sense of the soul hitherto in darkness without the divine light and blinded by its desires, is now such that its deep caverns, because of the divine union, 'with unwonted brightness give light and warmth together to the Beloved.'

With unwonted brightness give light and
warmth together to their Beloved.

87. These caverns of the soul's faculties being now in a wonderful way among the marvellous splendours of the lamps which burn within them, being lighted and burning in God, remit back to God in God, in addition to their self-surrender to Him, those very splendours which they receive from Him in loving bliss; they also, turning to God in God, being themselves lamps burning in the brightness of the divine lamps, return to the Beloved that very light and warmth of love which they receive from Him. Now, indeed, they give back unto Him, in the way they receive them, those very splendours which He communicates, as crystal reflects the rays of the sun; but in a nobler manner, because of the intervention of the will.

With unwonted brightness

88. That is, strange and surpassing all imagination and description. For the perfection of beauty wherein the soul restores to God what it has received from Him is now in conformity with that perfection wherewith the understanding – made one with that of God – received the divine wisdom: and the perfection wherewith the will restores to God in God that very goodness He gave it – for it was given only to be restored – is in conformity with that perfection wherein the will is united with the will of God. In the same way, proportional to the perfection of its knowledge of God's greatness, united therewith, does the soul shine and give forth the warmth of love. And according to the perfection of the other divine attributes

communicated to the soul, such as strength, beauty, justice, are those perfections wherewith the spiritual mind, now in enjoyment, gives back to the Beloved in the Beloved the very light and warmth which it is receiving from Him.

89. The soul now being one with God is itself God by participation, and though not so perfectly as it will be in the world to come, is still, as I have said, as God in a shadow. Thus, then, the soul, by reason of its transformation, being a shadow of God, effects through God in God what He effects within it Himself by Himself, because the will of both is one. And as God is giving Himself with a free and gracious will, so the soul also with a will, the more free and the more generous the more it is united with God in God, is, as it were, giving back to God – in that loving complacency with which it regards the divine essence and perfections – God Himself.

90. This is a mystic and affective gift of the soul to God, for then the soul seems in truth to have God for its own possession, and that it possesses Him, as His adopted child, by a right of ownership, by the free gift of Himself made unto it. The soul gives to the Beloved, Who is God Himself, what He had given to it. Herein it pays the whole debt, for the soul giveth as much voluntarily with inestimable joy and delight, giving the Holy Spirit as its own of its own free will, so that God may be loved as He deserves to be.

91. Herein consists the inestimable joy of the soul, for it sees that it offers to God what becomes Him in His Infinite Being. Though it be true that the soul cannot give God to God anew, because He is always Himself in Himself, still it does so, perfectly and wisely, giving all that He has given it in requital of His love; this is to give as it is given, and God is repaid by this gift of the soul; nothing less could repay Him. He receives this gift of the soul as if it were its own, with kindness and grace, in the sense I have explained; and in that gift He loves it anew, and gives Himself freely to it, and the soul also loves Him anew. Thus, there is in fact a mutual interchange of love between the soul and God in the conformity of the union, and in the matrimonial surrender, wherein the goods of both, that is the divine essence, are possessed by both together, in the voluntary giving up of

each to the other. God and the soul say, the one to the other, what the Son of God said to the Father, ' All My things are Thine, and Thine are Mine, and I am glorified in them.' This will be verified in the fruition of the next life without intermission, and is verified in the state of union when the soul's communion with God energizes in an act of love.

92. The soul can offer such a gift, though far greater than itself, just as he who possesses many kingdoms and nations as his own, though greater than he, can bestow them upon whom he will. This is the soul's great delight, that it sees itself giving unto God more than itself is worth, that it gives Himself to God so generously, as if God were its own, in that divine light and warmth of love which He Himself has given it. This is effected in the life to come through the light of glory and of love, and in this life by faith most enlightened and by love most enkindled. Thus it is that the deep caverns of sense, with unwonted brightness give light and heat together to the Beloved. I say together, because the communication of the Father and of the Son and of the Holy Ghost in the soul is one; they are the light and the fire of love therein.

93. I must here observe briefly on the perfection of beauty where-with the soul makes this gift. In the act of union, as the soul enjoys a certain image of fruition, caused by the union of the understanding and will in God, it makes this gift of God to God, and of itself to Him, in most wonderful ways; delighting itself therein, and constrained thereto. As to love, the soul stands before God in strange beauty, as to the shadow of fruition in the same way, and also as to praise and gratitude.

94. As to the first, which is love, the soul has three grand perfec-tions of beauty. It loves God by means of God. This is an admirable perfection, because, set on fire by the Holy Ghost, and having the Holy Ghost dwelling within it, it loves as the Father loves the Son, as it is written, 'that the love wherewith Thou hast loved Me, may be in them, and I in them.' The second perfection is that it loves God in God, for in this union the soul is vehemently absorbed in the love of God, and God communicates Himself with great vehemence to it.

The third perfection of beauty is that the soul now loves God for what He is; for it loves Him not merely because He is bountiful, good, and generous to it, but much more earnestly, because He is all this essentially in Himself.

95. There are also three perfections of beauty in that shadow of fruition, marvellously great. The first is that the soul enjoys God here, united with God Himself, for as the understanding of the soul is one with wisdom and goodness, and perceives so clearly – though not perfectly as in the life to come – it delights greatly in all these, clearly understood, as I said before. The second perfection of beauty is that the soul delights itself in God alone without the admixture of any created thing. The third is that it enjoys Him alone as He is, without the admixture of any selfish feeling, or of any created object.

96. There are also three principal perfections of beauty in the praise of God which the soul offers to Him in union. The first is that the soul offers it as an act of duty, because it recognizes this as the end of its creation; as it is written, 'This people have I formed for Myself, they shall show forth My praise.' The second is, that it praises Him for blessings received, and because of the joy it has in praising our Lord Who is so great. The third is, that it praises Him for what He is in Himself, for if the praises of God were unaccompanied by any pleasure at all, still it would praise Him because He is Who He is.

97. Gratitude also has three principal perfections. The first is, thanksgiving for all natural and spiritual blessings, and for all benefits received. The second is the great delight of praising God, in the way of thanksgiving, for the soul is moved with great vehemence in the act. The third is that the soul gives thanks unto God only because He is, which is much more efficacious and more delightful.

STANZA IV

How gently and how lovingly
Thou liest awake in my bosom,
Where Thou secretly dwellest alone;
And in thy sweet breathing,
Full of grace and glory,
How tenderly Thou fillest me with Thy love.

EXPLANATION

Here the soul turns towards the Bridegroom in great love, magnifying Him and giving Him thanks for two marvellous graces which He sometimes effects within the soul through its union with Himself. The soul, too, observes on the way He produces them and on their effects upon itself.

2. The first effect is the awakening of God in the soul, and that in gentleness and love. The second is the breathing of God in the soul, and that in grace and bliss given in that breathing. The effect of this upon the soul is to make it love Him sweetly and tenderly. The stanza therefore may be paraphrased as follows: O how gently and how lovingly dost Thou lie awake in the depth and centre of my soul, where Thou in secret and in silence alone, as its sole Lord, abidest, not only as in Thine own house or in Thine own chamber, but also as within my own bosom, in close and intimate union: O how gently and how lovingly! Sweet to me is Thy breathing in that awakening, for it is full of grace and glory. O with what tenderness dost Thou inspire me with love of Thee! The figure is borrowed from one awaking from sleep; and drawing his breath, for the soul in this state feels it to be so.

How gently and how lovingly
Thou liest awake in my bosom,

3. The awakenings of God in the soul are manifold, and so many

that were I to describe them I should never end. This awakening, to which the soul refers here, the work of the Son of God, is, in my opinion, of the highest kind, and the source of the greatest good to the soul. This awakening is a movement of the Word in the depth of the soul of such grandeur, authority and glory, and of such profound sweetness, that all the balsams, all the aromatic herbs and flowers of the world seem to be mingled and shaken together for the production of that sweetness: that all the kingdoms and dominions of the world, all the powers and virtues of heaven are moved; this is not the whole, all the virtues, substance, perfections and graces of all created things, shine forth and make the same movement in unison together. For as St John saith, 'What was made in Him was life,' and in Him moves and lives; as the Apostle says, 'In Him we live and move and are.'

4. The reason is this: when the grand Emperor would reveal Himself to the soul, moving Himself in the light He gives, and yet not moving in it – He, upon whose shoulder is the principality, that is, the three worlds of heaven, earth, and hell, and all that is in them, and Who sustains all by the word of His power – then all seem to move together. As when the earth moves, all natural things upon it move with it; so is it when the Prince moves, for He carries his court, not the court Him. This, however, is an exceedingly imperfect illustration; for here not only all seem to move, but also to manifest their being, their beauty, power, and loveliness, the root of their duration and life in Him. There, indeed, the soul sees how all creatures, higher and lower, live, continue, and energize in Him, and understands the words of the Wise Man, 'by me kings reign . . . by me princes rule, and the mighty decree justice.'

5. Though it is true that the soul here sees that all these things are distinct from God, in that they have a created existence; it understands them in Him with their force, origin and strength, it knows also that God in His own essence is, in an infinitely pre-eminent way, all these things, so that it understands them better in Him, their First Cause, than in themselves. This is the great joy of this awakening, namely, to know creatures in God, and not God in His creatures: this is to know effects in their cause, and not cause by its effects.

6. This movement in the soul is wonderful, for God Himself moves not. Without movement on the part of God, the soul is renewed and moved by Him; the divine life and being and the harmony of creation are revealed with marvellous newness, the cause assuming the designation of the effect resulting from it. If we regard the effect, we may say with the Wise Man that God moves, 'for wisdom is more moveable than all moveable things', not because it moves itself but because it is the source and principle of all motion, and 'permanently in herself, she reneweth all things'; this is the meaning of the words, 'more moveable than all moveable things'.

7. Thus, then, strictly speaking, in this movement it is the soul that is moved and awakened, and the expression 'awake' is correct. God however being always, as the soul sees Him, the mover, the ruler, and the giver of life, power, graces, and gifts to all creatures, contains all in Himself, virtually, actually, and supremely. The soul beholds what God is in Himself, and what He is in creatures. So may we see, when the palace is thrown open, in one glance, both the magnificence of him who inhabits it, and what he is doing. This, according to my understanding of it, is this awakening and vision of the soul; it is as if God drew back some of the many veils and coverings that are before it, so that it might see what He is; then indeed – but still dimly, because all the veils are not drawn back, that of faith remaining – the divine face full of grace bursts through and shines, which, as it moves all things by its power, appears together with the effect it produces, and this is the awakening of the soul.

8. Though all that is good in man comes from God, and though man of himself can do nothing that is good, it may be said in truth, that our awakening is the awakening of God, and our rising the rising of God. 'Arise, why sleepest Thou, O Lord?' saith the Psalmist. That is in effect to say, Raise us up and awake us, for we are fallen and asleep. Thus then, because the soul had fallen asleep, and could never rouse itself again, and because it is God alone who can open its eyes, and effect its awakening, this awakening is most properly referred to God: 'Thou awakest in my bosom.'

Thou awakest in my bosom,

9. Awake us, O Lord, and enlighten us, that we may know and love the good things which Thou hast set always before us, and we shall know that Thou art moved to do us good, and hast had us in remembrance. It is utterly impossible to describe what the soul, in this awakening, knows and feels of the majesty of God, in the inmost depths of its being, that is, its bosom. For in the soul resounds an infinite power, with the voice of a multitude of perfections, of thousands and thousands of virtues, wherein itself abiding and subsisting, becomes 'terrible as an army set in array', sweet and gracious in Him who comprehends in Himself all the sweetness, and all the graces of His creation.

10. But here comes the question, how can the soul bear so vehement a communication while in the flesh, when in truth it has not strength for it without fainting away? The mere sight of Assuerus on his throne, in his royal robe, glittering with gold and precious stones, was so terrible in the eyes of Esther, that she fainted through fear, so awful was his face. 'I saw Thee, my Lord, as an angel of God, and my heart was troubled, for fear of thy glory.' Glory oppresses him who beholds it, if it does not glorify him. How much more then is the soul now liable to faint away, when it beholds not an angel but God Himself, the Lord of the angels, with His face full of the beauty of all creatures, of terrible power and glory, and the voice of the multitude of His perfections. It is to this that Job referred when he said, 'We have heard scarce a little drop of His word; who shall be able to behold the thunder of His greatness?' and again, 'I will not that He contend with me with much strength, nor that He oppress me with the weight of His greatness.'

11. The soul, however, does not faint away and tremble at this awakening so powerful and glorious. There are two reasons for this: one is that it is now in the state of perfection, and therefore the lower portion of it is purified and conformed to the spirit, exempt from that pain and loss which spiritual communications involve, when the sense and spirit are not purified and disposed for the reception of them. 2. The second and the principal reason is that referred to in

the first line of this stanza, namely, that God shows Himself gentle and loving. For as He shows His greatness and glory to the soul in order to comfort and exalt it, so does He favour and strengthen it also, and sustain its natural powers while manifesting His greatness gently and lovingly. This is easy enough to Him, Who with His right hand protected Moses that he might behold His glory.

12. Thus the soul feels God's love and gentleness to be commensurate with His power, authority, and greatness, for in Him these are all one. Its delight is therefore vehement, and the protection it receives strong in gentleness and love, so that itself being made strong may be able without fainting away to sustain this vehement joy. Esther, indeed, fainted away, but that was because the king seemed unfavourable towards her, for with 'burning eyes' he 'showed the wrath of his breast', but the moment he looked graciously upon her, touched her with his sceptre and kissed her, she recovered herself, for he had said to her, 'I am thy brother, fear not.'

13. So is it with the soul in the presence of the King of kings, for the moment He shows Himself as its Bridegroom and Brother, all fear vanishes away. Because in showing unto it, in gentleness and not in anger, the strength of His power and the love of His goodness, He communicates to it the strength and love of His breast, 'leaping from His throne' to caress it, as the bridegroom from his secret chamber, touching it with the sceptre of His majesty, and as a brother embracing it. There the royal robes and the fragrance thereof, which are the marvellous attributes of God; there the splendour of gold which is charity, and the glittering of the precious stones of supernatural knowledge; and there the face of the Word full of grace, strike the queenly soul, so that, transformed in the virtues of the King of heaven, it beholds itself a queen: with the Psalmist, therefore, may it be said of it, and with truth, 'The queen stood on Thy right hand in gilded clothing, surrounded with variety.' And as all this passes in the very depths of the soul, it is added immediately, 'Where Thou secretly dwellest alone.'

Where Thou secretly dwellest alone,

14. He is said to dwell secretly in the soul's bosom, because, as I have said, this sweet embracing takes place in the inmost substance and powers of the soul. We must keep in mind that God dwells in a secret and hidden way in all souls, in their very substance, for if He did not, they could not exist at all. This dwelling of God is very different in different souls; in some He dwells alone, in others not; in some He dwells contented, in others displeased; in some as in His own house, giving His orders, and ruling it; in others, as a stranger in a house not His own, where He is not permitted to command, or to do anything at all. Where personal desires and self-will least abound, there is He most alone, most contented, there He dwells as in His own house, ruling and directing it, and the more secretly He dwells, the more He is alone.

15. So then in that soul wherein no desire dwells, and out of which all images and forms of created things have been cast, the Beloved dwells most secretly Himself, and the purer the soul and the greater its estrangement from everything but God, the more intimate His converse and the closer His embrace. He dwells there then in secret, for Satan cannot come near His dwelling place, nor see the embracing; nor can any understanding explain it. But He is not hidden from the soul in the state of perfection, for such a soul is ever conscious of His presence. Only in these awakenings He seems to awake Who before was asleep in the soul's bosom; and though it felt and enjoyed His presence, He seemed as one sleeping within.

16. O how blessed is that soul which is ever conscious of God reposing and resting within it. How necessary it is for such a soul to flee from the matters of this world, to live in great tranquillity, so that nothing whatever shall disturb the Beloved 'at His repose'.

17. He is there as it were asleep in the embraces of the soul, and the soul is, in general, conscious of His presence, and, in general, delights exceedingly in it. If He were always awake in the soul, the communications of knowledge and love would be unceasing, and that would be a state of glory. If He awakes but once, merely opening His eyes, and affects the soul so profoundly, what would become of it if He were continually awake within it?

18. He dwells secretly in other souls, those which have not attained to this state of union, not indeed displeased, though they are not yet perfectly disposed for union: these souls in general are not conscious of His presence, but only during the time of these sweet awakenings, which however are not of the same kind with those already described, neither indeed are they to be compared with them. But the state of these souls is not so secret from the devil, nor so far above the reach of the understanding as the other, because the senses always furnish some indications of it by the excitement into which they are thrown. The senses are not perfectly annihilated before the union is complete, and they manifest their power in some degree, because they are not yet wholly spiritual. But in this awakening of the Bridegroom in the perfect soul, all is perfect because He effects it all Himself in the way I have spoken of. In this awakening, as of one aroused from sleep and drawing breath, the soul feels the breathing of God, and therefore it says: 'In Thy sweet breathing.'

> *And in Thy sweet breathing,*
> *full of grace and glory,*
> *How tenderly*
> *Thou fillest me with Thy love.*

19. I would not speak of this breathing of God, neither do I wish to do so, because I am certain that I cannot; and indeed were I to speak of it, it would seem then to be something less than what it is in reality. This breathing of God is in the soul, in which in the awakening of the deep knowledge of the Divinity, He breathes the Holy Ghost according to the measure of that knowledge which absorbs it most profoundly, which inspires it most tenderly with love according to what it saw. This breathing is full of grace and glory, and therefore the Holy Ghost fills the soul with goodness and glory, whereby He inspires it with the love of Himself, transcending all glory and all understanding. This is the reason why I say nothing more.

THE PILGRIM'S PROGRESS

John Bunyan

Written in prison, where Bunyan had been sent for unauthorized preaching, and first published in 1678, this classic story has been described as the most popular work of Christian spirituality written in English, and as the first English novel. It describes the road to the Celestial City, by way of Doubting Castle, the Delectable Mountains, Vanity Fair and other places whose names have entered the very fabric of the language.

Fascinating as literature, entertaining as story, profound as spiritual teaching for the soul's journey, *The Pilgrim's Progress* is 'a masterpiece which generation after generation of ordinary men and women have taken to their hearts' (Hugh Ross Williamson).

Fount Classics
BIOGRAPHY

JOHN BUNYAN
The Christian
Gordon Wakefield

John Bunyan, born in 1628 son of a Bedford tinker, and teenage soldier in the army of Robert Cromwell, fell into a kind of religious madness and emerged from this a soldier in the army of Christ: a fiery preacher in the radical Puritan tradition. His fervour brought him into conflict with the Restoration government, and he spent much time in prison. It was there he wrote his famous masterpiece, *The Pilgrim's Progress*. By the time of his death he had written some sixty works.

This outstanding biography takes Bunyan seriously as a spiritual guide, and sets his life in the context of the history of English Christianity, as well as the political conflicts of his time.

Gordon Wakefield was Principal of the Queen's College Birmingham from 1979 until his retirement in 1987. He is a Methodist minister and director of the Alister Hardy Centre for Research into Religious Experience. He edited *A Dictionary of Christian Spirituality* (SCM) and, in 1986, was the first Methodist minister to be awarded the Lambeth doctorate of divinity. He lives in Lichfield

'Wakefield's excellent book helps us to understand why Bunyan's influence continues down the centuries and across the continents' *Baptist Times*

'The chief merit of this impressive theological life is to bring back a Bunyan with a vibrant word for now, one that leaps all denominational frontiers'
Methodist Recorder

AUTOBIOGRAPHY OF A SAINT
St Thérèse of Lisieux
Translated by Ronald Knox

St Thérèse of Lisieux, known as the 'Little Flower', who died in 1897 virtually unknown outside her convent, is now recognized as the most popular and influential saint of our times. She was canonized in 1925, and successive Popes have recommended her as an authoritative spiritual guide for the twentieth century and beyond.

The immense popularity of Térèse is largely based upon this book. It is her own personal testimony. Written at odd moments in school exercise books and on scraps of paper, it gives a vivid human account of the life of a saint from the inside; intimate, spontaneous and sparkling throughout with a delightful humour.

Ronald Knox was a witty and brilliant Anglican priest and scholar who became one of this century's most famous converts to Roman Catholicism, and went on in the 1940s to make one of the greatest modern translations of the Bible.

THÉRÈSE OF LISIEUX

Michael Hollings

The most influential and most popular saint of modern times, Térèse Martin died virtually unknown outside her Carmelite convent in 1897, at the age of 24. After her death came the storm of glory, the miracles and the acclaim that swept her statue into every church and her spiritual teaching into the mouths of Popes.
Thérèse's 'little way' of prayer was a message for humanity of our time, and the publication of her own writings made it known around the world. This vivid biography brings the reader into the closest contact with the life and world of Thérèse, often in her own words, and serves as an ideal introduction to this 'little' mystic who inspires millions of Christians.

Michael Hollings is Roman Catholic parish priest of St Mary of the Angels, Moorhouse Road, Bayswater.

'. . . a gem of brief and yet deep biography . . . an account which is sensitive and totally dispels any preconceived notion of sentimentality in connection with 'the Little Flower'. Father Hollings comments with great understanding on her writings and special contribution to spirituality . . . It is by far the best book I have ever seen on this extraordinary woman' *Methodist Recorder*